BRANDON'S WINDOW

A Grandmother's Documentary of Reversing Autism Naturally

BRANDON'S WINDOW

A Grandmother's Documentary of Reversing Autism Naturally

by

Lynne M. George

A PREMIER MARK PRODUCTION

ISBN: 978-0-578-00383-2
Copyright © by Lynne M. George (Pending)

Credits   Brandon's Window Video: Wal-Mart
Brandon's Window Video and Book: Chuck E. Cheese
Brandon's Window Book: Burger King
Brandon's Window Book: Disney World
Brandon's Window Book (Television): Teletubbies, Wow Wow Wubbzy, Backyardigans, Wonder Pets, Word Girl, Sesame Street, Barney, Super Why, Curious George, Clifford, Dragon Tales
Brandon's Window Book (and Video) (Products): Cheetos, Pull-Ups, V-Tech, Fisher Price, Leap Frog, V-Smile, Learning Resources
Brandon's Window Video (and Book) (Clothing): Nike, Old Navy, Marvel Comics' Spider Man

Lynne M. George/BRANT, LLC
Book's development
Book's co-editor
Book's photograph (front cover)
Video's producer
Video's director
Video's narrator
Video's co-editor

Melody George/PREMIER MARK and BRANT, LLC
Book's development
Book's co-editor
Book's photograph (author pix/back cover)
Book's designer
Book's production editor
Book's cover designer (back/front covers)
Book's graphics/illustrator
Book's radio show transcriptions (appendix)
Video's co-editor

CONTACT INFORMATION

Author's Information:
Lynne M. George
BRANT, LLC
P.O. Box 1617
Gray, Louisiana 70359
USA
E-mail: brandonswindow@yahoo.com
website: www.brandonswindow.com

Book Producer's Information:
Melody George
PREMIER MARK
website: www.brandonswindow.com

For correlating videos, visit YouTube.com: Brandon's Window.

To my beautiful grandsons, Anthony and Brandon, you are my inspiration as to why I am writing this book. To my loving son and daughter-in-law, Tony and LaShon, continue being the terrific parents that you are. May God continue to bless you. To my Mother and Father, I love you guys so much. Thank you for instilling in me the determination to never give up. Thank you for always being there for me. I am truly blessed, at this point in time, to still have you among the land of the living. I love you with all my heart, and I thank God for you every day. To my siblings—Kenneth, Noel Jr., Lorin, Melody and Pam—continue to be the Godly men and women that you are. I love you with all my heart. To my in-laws, Penny, Debbie, Sharon and Sterling, God bless you and I love you. To my nieces and nephews—BJ, Linda, Marques, Courtney, Brittany, Matthew, Terez, Noelle, Tre and Trent—continue striving for excellence, and keep God in your life. To my aunts and uncles—Aunt Ophelia, Uncle Wilbert, Aunt Mary, Jessie Mae, T-Bea, Auntie Clara, Uncle Ted & Auntie Marie, Auntie Cynthia, Uncle Al & Aunt Shirley, Uncle Ralph & Aunt Joel, Uncle Frank & T-Norma, may God bless and keep you. To cousins—L'il Bill & Deb, Ernest & June, Nena, Lori, Barry, Terri, L'il Al & Holly, Jeff, Anya, Tanya & Tracy, Marc Le. & Janine, Monique, Simone & Marc S., Quincy, Anna Marie & Chris, Chris G., James, John-Michael & Lynn, Robin, Marc La., Teddy Jr. & Michelle, Thais, Pia, Dre' (my other son) & Suzette, Shannon, L'il Ernest, Kris, Allison, Reka, Tiffany, Luca, Bobbie Jean, Trixie, Donna, Lisa, Mary Louise, Tamika, Jimmy W., Kevin K., Renee, Buffy, Arch Van Meter, Lois Simpson, Glen Lord, Godfrey LeBouef, Martha & Roy, the Keigers and a host of cousins, family and friends— love you guys! To my friends Ezella, Ginger, Robert, Flip, Doris, Tina, Sybil, Candice, Loretta, Diane, Wanda, Anita, Juanita, Dwayne, Dena, Diondria, Marie, Kim, Mel, Adam, Terry, Carla & Fly., Kathy, Ronnie, Mamie, Levi, Sonja, Dawn, Nikitra, Brenda, Aneka, Amy, Donyell, Asia, India, Nolan Jr. and Jimmy Jack, Ken & Phyllis, Cornell, MJS, Chuck W., George R., Richard B., Berniece, Rhonda, Monica, Mona, Noelee, Roxanne & Robert, Gwen & Leslie, Joe & Fran, Martin F., Dr. Scott, Dr. Deepak, Dr. Kara, Thibodaux Chiropractic, Flynn Chiropractic, Thibodaux School Board, St. Lucy, St. Francis, Vandebilt Class of 1975, Nicholls State, Sixth Ward Middle Faculty (2002-2003), Angie, Diane and Rosalyn, thank you for being there for me. To Brandon's Early Steps' Speech Therapists—Ms. B. Trahan, Ms. B. Wallis, et al.; his teachers at Head Start and Terrebonne Parish Special Education Department/Oakshire—Ms. K. Scott, Ms. Wendy, et al.; Dekalb County Special Education Department and staff, thank you for helping for your dedication in educating Brandon. To the Deweyville community and members of the Plymouth Rock Baptist Church and Emmanuel Missionary Baptist Church (East Houma), thank for being my extended family. To Shirley "Grandmommie" and Uncle Charles Brown, Zach and Zaria, Great & Aunt Ira, thank you for welcoming me into the family. To Grandmother "Bev" (thanks for helping me raise a fine young man), PawPaw & Joyce, Pops & Ms. Sandra, Mike & Pudgy, Mikey & Laura, John, Johnny, Joseph and Jason, et al., from the bottom of my heart, thank you!!! To Herbert & Lizzie Mae and the rest of the Guidry family, you all have been so wonderful, and I love you.
If anyone was left out, it was not intentional.

*In memory of my grandmother, Bessie James Lewis, and
my aunt, Betty Rose Lewis Brown—my guardian angels…
I can always feel your presence.*

ENDORSEMENTS AND CREDITS

Special thanks to:

Dr. Natasha Campbell-McBride, "Gut and Psychology Syndrome" ("GAPS"), thank you for allowing me to reference GAPS in "Brandon's Window." Your book has empowered and equipped our family with the knowledge and tools to reverse Brandon's autism.

Dr. Chris Greene "Wake Up To Nutrition"/"Dr. Chris' Natural Pharmacy", thank you for taking a personal interest in Brandon by holding our hand and guiding us with your knowledge of natural nutrition and whole food supplementation.

Both of you have played such integral parts in our journey of reversing Brandon's autism naturally. May God continue to bless you.

DR. CHRIS GREENE:

Wake Up To Nutrition
By Dr. Chris Greene

Call Toll Free:
1-877-7AWAKEN

Dr. Chris was born in Decatur, Georgia in late 1962. During his childhood, his parents, David and Dorothy, opened a health food store in Tucker called "Mother Nature's Market." In helping his parents run the business, Dr. Chris' education in natural medicine had begun. While attending Chiropractic College, he had several jobs where he could exercise his budding talent in natural medicine. In 1994, Dr. Chris graduated from Life University. Dr. Chris decided to open his first Chiropractic office, "Healing Hands," in 1998. The name soon became synonymous with Dr. Chris himself. Dr. Chris' personal quest for knowledge never subsided. Having questioned the nutritional industry, Dr. Chris began to study more into the topic of whole food verses synthetic supplements. He began to realize that most supplements on the market were synthetically isolated and lacked many cofactors needed for proper utilization. These "manmade" vitamins did not even come from food sources. The frustration with the industry caused him to close his office in 2002 and go back to Mother Nature's Market where he acted as co-owner and provided nutritional consultations. Here he attempted to educate consumers on the atrocities being committed within the health food industry. However, this was not enough. In 2004, he started a radio show to raise public awareness of whole food supplementation. "Wake Up to Nutrition" airs daily from 11 AM-12 PM on AM 1010. As the show grew, Dr. Chris decided to open his own store—"Dr. Chris' Natural Pharmacy"—in 2005. The store features whole food supplementation, BioMeridian Scanning, and of course, consultations with Dr. Chris himself. And now with the opening of www.wakeuptonutrition.com, listeners can download past shows and purchase all the products they hear about from the online store.

Dr. Chris' Natural Pharmacy
1982 E. Main Street/Hwy. 78, #D
Snellville, GA 30078
Phone: (770) 979-5125
Fax: (770) 979-6911
Mail Order: (770) 979-5825
Website: www.wakeuptonutrition.com
"The Most Innovative Nutrition Provider Online!"

Live on the Internet:
"To Your Health with Dr. Chris Greene"
WGUN Ten. Click on "Listen Live" button
Radio 1010 AM (Mon.- Fri., 11:00 am to 12:00 pm - EST)
Call-in Number: (770) 491-7748

DR. NATASHA CAMPBELL-MCBRIDE:

Dr. Natasha Campbell-McBride is the author of "Gut and Psychology Syndrome—Natural treatment for Dyspraxia, Autism, A.D.D., Dyslexia, A.D.H.D., Depression and Schizophrenia." To purchase Gut and Psychology Syndrome ("GAP"), please contact: Laurie Ledbetter laurieledbetter@guthealth.info or Dr. Chris' Natural Pharmacy www.wakeuptonutrition.com.

Dr. Natasha Campbell-McBride
"Gut and Psychology Syndrome"

Dr. Natasha Campbell-McBride set up the Cambridge Nutrition Clinic in 1998. As a parent of a child diagnosed with learning disabilities, she was acutely aware of the difficulties facing other parents like her, and she has devoted much of her time to helping these families. She realised that nutrition played a critical role in helping children and adults to overcome their disabilities, and has pioneered the use of probiotics in this field.

Her willingness to share her knowledge has resulted in her contributing to many publications, as well as presenting at numerous seminars and conferences on the subjects of learning disabilities and digestive disorders. This book "Gut and Psychology Syndrome" captures her experience and knowledge, incorporating her most recent work.

She believes that the link between learning disabilities, the food and drink that we take, and the condition of our digestive system is absolute, and the results of her work have supported her position on this subject. In her clinic, parents discuss all aspects of their child's condition, confident in the knowledge that they are not only talking to a professional but to a parent who has lived their experience. Her deep understanding of the challenges they face, puts her advice in a class of its own.

Natasha Campbell-McBride holds a Degree in Medicine and Postgraduate Degrees in both Neurology and Human Nutrition. In her Clinic in Cambridge she specialises in Nutrition for Children and Adults with Behavioural and Learning Disabilities, and Adults with Digestive and Immune System Disorders.

Learn more about Dr. Natasha Campbell-McBride's take on autism. (*See* "You Tube Videos/Corganic TV, Autism Diet: Donna Gates and Dr. Campbell-McBride" (Videos 1-6)).

LAURIE LEDBETTER:

Laurie Ledbetter
US Distributor for
 Dr. Natasha Campbell-McBride
GUT AND PSYCHOLOGY
P.O. Box 418
Pinelake, GA 30072
Phone: (404) 298-9188
Website: http://www.guthealth.info

SHIRLEY BROWN:

Brandon's Pizza

CHARLES BROWN:

Brandon's Lemonade
Brandon's Breakfast Juice

MELODY GEORGE:

Melody George
PREMIER MARK
Phone: 1-866-972-7268
www.brandonswindow.com

Melody George

Melody George is the sister of Lynne George. She is an Administrative Assistant for an International Fortune 500 Law Firm. Melody is a poet, author of "Life is Worth Living" – ISBN: 0-595-31884-3, family historian and mother.

INTRODUCTION

This journal began when a strange twist of faith turned a once healthy, young grandmother's world completely around. She became permanently disabled with a debilitating back injury as the result of a car accident in 2003. Her pain was 24/7. And, on a scale of 1 to 10, the pain registered 15. She had endured unrelenting back and leg pains which did not allow her to sleep, sit or stand. She could not do small tasks such as opening doors or picking up a simple item. Her independence was diminished. There were times when she was on the verge of giving up, but her parents reassured her that *with God's grace, things would get better.* She learned to persevere, endure and press on for the sake of her family, and, most importantly, for her son, daughter-in-law and their two young children. Ironically, her younger grandson, Brandon, seemed oblivious to anything. At a stage of her suffering, she discovered *something different* about Brandon. Her once precious, responsive and energetic grandson's temperament had changed. Soon after, he was diagnosed with autism.

TABLE OF CONTENTS

CHAPTER 1—
EXPECTATIONS

November 2002

> *"Everything seemed to be on task…. Then, the milestone—old and new—just stopped."*

17 months

A precious moment in any grandmother's eyes—the birth of my second grandson—Brandon. With the usual expectations—ten fingers, ten toes—Brandon was a beautiful, healthy baby in every way. As the months passed, we found the usual expectations and "milestones" for any baby. Everything seemed to be on task. He sat up, crawled, grunted, mumbled and even said "bye-bye." Then, the milestones—old and new—just stopped. He walked at 13 months, but my grandson was a walking "zombie." Not fully comprehending what was happening to Brandon, we, however, noticed that he walked on his tip-toes. We also noticed things on television excited him. He drooled with his mouth opened in an "O" shape. When he jumped with such excitement, you could see his heart beat through his shirt. But, somehow, no matter how hard he tried, no words came from his mouth. Our family and friends began to notice a change in Brandon. He gazed out of our glass door with no emotion—no expression. He seemed not to recognize or interact socially with immediate family members. This straying-from-the-norm pattern began to be more and more prevalent. **Help!** *Were we losing our beautiful baby?*

We took Brandon to his pediatrician. It was there we first heard the word "autistic". I was somewhat familiar with the term "autism", but it never hit close to home. I did not understand what autism entailed nor did I fathom what impact autism would have on our family. I knew my grandson was slipping away, and I was diligent to help him. I researched the internet and printed any and all articles about autism. I read pages upon pages from my bed on an odyssey for Brandon's cure.

According to Brandon's pediatrician, he was not on task for his age. We presented his doctor with a battery of questions to identify and discuss the peculiar things Brandon would do. We also discussed Brandon's poor eating habits. It was difficult to get him to eat any **nutritious food**. Although, he craved mostly junk food—*Cheetos®*, pizza, bread and/or oatmeal cream pies—he ate bite-sized pieces of bananas from our hands. We attempted to spoon-feed him, which only resulted with an immediate gag reflex and projectile vomiting.

(Below is an excerpt from "Gut and Psychology Syndrome," by Dr. Natasha Campbell-McBride, page 158.)

> There are some contributory factors. For example, any secretion from the body is a way of eliminating toxins. Saliva is one of them. GAPS patients have very toxic bodies and some of those toxins get excreted through saliva. This contributes to the toxic load in the mouth, altering the taste and feel of foods.

> *"[T]oxic load... altering the taste and feel of foods."*

We later bottle-fed him and cleverly slipped crushed vitamins through a pabulum-like formula. Brandon's mother gave him chocolate milk which promoted bowel movement; otherwise, he suffered from constipation. His pediatrician, however, seemed to dismiss Brandon's poor eating habits and responded, "as long as he was eating, these bad eating habits would change" as he grew older. When we returned home, we attempted Brandon's spoon-feeding again which gave no new results. For most people, feeding times would generally be a joyful occasion, but for us, it turned into a highly-frustrating ordeal. Brandon's reaction was as though we were killing him when he sat in his high chair to eat. Soon after, the idea of the spoon-feedings diminished.

A PLEASANT SURPRISE!

Year Two
"CHRISTMAS"

"Maybe I am reaching him."

At Brandon's second Christmas, I was extremely elated when I saw him place one giant building block on top of another. *I image everyone in the house must have thought I was crazy when I screamed with excitement, but they were oblivious to the fact that I had been trying to teach him to do this task for several months.* And, he finally did it! I thought... *Maybe I am reaching him.* At best, Brandon's accomplishment was my glimpse of hope for me. Before, he seemed to be in his own world. But, if anything, I praised this accomplishment. He finally did it! I was willing and ready to try something new. *Maybe there was another window of opportunity to reach him.*

Age 2½

At two and one-half years of age, Brandon still did not talk; he rocked back and forth to music. Since music seemed to stimulate him, I attempted to introduce his learning through songs, such as ABC's, prayers, etc. Nevertheless, Brandon never said the words his parents longed to hear—"Mommy and Daddy." He, however, began to "parrot talk", and he loved television shows like *Barney* and *Teletubbies*.

CHAPTER 2—
EARLY STEPS

> *"Early Steps prepared all the necessary documents... ."*

*2 years,
7 months*

> *"[I]mplement certain strategies and ideas which would introduce Brandon to new things and new places."*

EARLY INTERVENTION IS THE KEY!

In July 2004, Brandon was referred to the Louisiana's Early Intervention System— ("Early Steps"). Early Steps (was *dedicated to empower families who have children from the ages of 18 months to three years with disabilities and/or developmental delays.* The Specialist Intake Coordinator assessed Brandon with an *18 Month "Ages and Stages" Questionnaire.* (*See* **APPENDIX A**: Early Steps.)

Fortunately, Early Steps prepared all of the necessary documents, applications, testing(s), evaluations and Medicaid application. The process of the qualification/acceptance took one year (June 2004 to June 2005).

Early Steps allowed Brandon to have four devoted in-home teachers: Ms. Trahan (speech pathologist), Ms. Wallis (special instructor), Ms. Chase (speech therapist), Ms. Wednesday (occupational therapist), in addition to an intake coordinator and a family service coordinator. Once a month, the supervisors of Early Steps visited our home to evaluate and document Brandon's progress.

At age two years, seven months, Early Steps suggested that Brandon's family members implement certain strategies and ideas which would introduce him to new things and new places. Brandon's monthly progress with Early Steps was measured through notes, direct observation and parent reports. In one month's time, Brandon was able to follow simple commands, such as turning pages of a book. He said six to seven words. However, he still babbled during play and repeated words or phrases. Early Steps observed and documented that Brandon "liked" affection. Although Brandon was a picky eater, he began finger-feeding himself and continued to prefer his bottle.

Brandon's Speech Pathologist (Ms. Trahan) informed us that he demonstrated a developmental delay in the areas of receptive and expressive language skills. (*See* **APPENDIX B**: Terrebonne Parish Special Education Department)

CHAPTER 3—
THE BIG
TRANSITION
(AGE 3)

The BiG Transition
Head Start Through the
Special Education Department

Once Brandon turned three, the Special Education representative (Ms. Linda) met with us to discuss services regarding his transition to the Head Start Program ("Head Start"). The Special Education Department also provided resources and information regarding autism. Brandon's family and the Early Steps' team participated in the transition meetings.

When Brandon reached his third birthday, it was time to be bussed to the nearest elementary school which implemented the Head Start/Early Steps programs.

Ms. Belinda's report *(excerpt)*:

At this stage, Brandon spoke spontaneously, using simple one-syllable words.

Ms. Barbara's report *(excerpt)*:

Brandon also attempted some work approximations.

The family's report *(excerpt)*:

Brandon moves easily. He is a true boy. He runs, jumps, walks, climbs, and scoots on the floor. He sees fine—far away and close. Brandon comes when you call him, and he acknowledges his name. To communicate, Brandon will pull you to what he wants. Brandon moods: He cries when he is frustrated and sad. When he is happy, he laughs and plays. The main concern is he is unable to adjust to new things. Brandon finger feeds himself and now uses a sippy cup. Though he is not potty trained, he is starting to understand the potty concept. He doesn't mind us taking him for number 1; but, he will not sit on the toilet for number 2. He pulls the toilet seat up and down and screams as you put him on the potty, but he will sit on the toilet when the toilet lid is closed. He uses his own imagination. He knows where his toys are. He knows how to turn the TV on and off. He likes to play chase. Brandon's eating habits are of concern. And, we continue to work on the potty training. Brandon repeats some nursery rhymes, numbers and alphabets. Much improvement is noted. Brandon benefited from the team's collaboration, with everyone being on the same page, through monthly meetings and quarterly reports.

Age 3

"Brandon attended the ... School.... [H]e did not ride on his brother's school bus."

HOMEwork

"At home, we devised signals... ."

"[O]ur family needed to help Brandon with social skills."

"Brandon walked on his toes..."

At this period, Brandon was age three and ready for Head Start.

In the meantime, we realized the difficulty of taking Brandon to movies, restaurants, church, shopping—basically anywhere. He was disruptive and drew attention. We, however, learned to adjust. When Brandon became disruptive, we calmly talked and escorted him away from the activities which excited him. Regardless of the invitation, whenever kids were allowed, we included him. Again, we adjusted!

Brandon attended the Oakshire Elementary School along with his kindergartener brother. Ironically, he did not ride his brother's school bus. He was transported to and from school in the special education bus. Ms. Scott (teacher) and Ms. Wendy (paraprofessional) patiently worked with him.

Brandon's class consisted of eight students— all experiencing learning disabilities. He was finally in the surroundings of his peers, but he had difficulty sitting still and continued to isolate himself from the rest of the class.

HOMEWORK

At home, we devised signals for Brandon, such as tapping the back of our hands to suggest "no" or "stop." As we said the word(s), we motioned for him either to take our hand or to stand close to us. The realization that Brandon might not function intellectually crossed our minds. If this assessment were correct, our family needed to help Brandon with his social skills. We found it helpful to continue to take Brandon to restaurants with play areas. For several months, he just walked around the play area, stared outside, observed passing cars and flapped his arms with excitement.

When Brandon walked on his toes in his socks, he could not climb in the play areas. I asked the manager if Brandon could wear his sneakers while playing. He complied.

I implemented directives for Brandon pertaining to the play areas which took several weeks. Soon after, Brandon was able to follow his brother little-by-little up the stairs, through the tunnels and down the slides. What an accomplishment! Instead of stimming, he played like other kids—without conversation—without any sounds of excitement.

On another occasion, Brandon flapped his arms in a department store. His stimming caught the attention of the store clerk. She looked at me as though I should reprimand him in some manner. I expressed, "This is my grandson, Brandon. He has autism." She replied, "Oh, I'm so sorry." I responded, "Well, I'm not, because he is a wonderful and beautiful child." Another lady overheard us talking and approached me and said, "I overheard your conversation with the clerk. I think my five-year-old son has autism, but everyone in my family is in denial. So he's not getting any help." She told me she heard peace, love and acceptance in my voice when I spoke of Brandon. Her assessment was definitely true. I told her that I believed in the saying, "It takes a village to raise a child"… especially a child with special needs. I expressed that she was not alone. I informed her to: 1) address the situation with early intervention—through education; and 2) collectively get her family on the same page regarding her child's wellbeing. The lady thanked me and said that my testimony gave her the strength to face her family and seek help for her child.

My motto: *When God closes a door, he always opens a window.* And, when life gives you lemons, you make lemonade.

"God, please grant Brandon a good life."

> *"Another lady overhead us ... and said, ... "I think my five-year-old son has autism, but everyone in my family is in denial."*

> *"'It takes a village to raise a child'... especially one with special needs... . I informed her ... early intervention—through education; and ... collectively get her family on the same page."*

> *"When God closes a door, he always opens a window."*

> *"[T]hese stimming and flapping cycles had to be broken."*

> *"[C]hanges in Brandon's life ... was almost like going against a force of nature."*

The Departure

> *"[R]eturned to ... Atlanta....*
>
> *[A]ssistance followed."*

Brandon played with his toys in an unconventional way. He would spin the wheels of an item or even himself. He continuously opened and closed doors or turned on and off light switches. When objects were placed in a specific order, he got upset if those particular objects were moved. Also, if Brandon saw people seated in a certain order, regardless if they were strangers, he grew upset to the point of tears and attempted to reposition them in the order he recalled.

Brandon drooled and flapped his arms with excitement whenever he saw fans in motion. We unanimously determined these stimming and flapping cycles had to be broken; therefore, the "Clap. No flap." substitution was implemented.

Brandon's delayed development made it difficult for us to communicate with him. It seemed as though we spoke a foreign language. In addition, he functioned almost "zombie-like". We were unable to read any facial expressions. However, we recognized almost instantly when Brandon was sleepy, because he banged his head on soft objects, such as the sofa, chairs or pillows until he fell asleep. Brandon cried for everything—that language was a similar, intense tone because he was unable to speak. We attempted to make changes in Brandon's life. For example, the move from the bottle to the sippy cup was almost like going against a force of nature. Brandon emphatically was not having it!

THE DEPARTURE

Shortly after my daughter-in-law's college graduation, the family returned to the Atlanta area. As in Louisiana, Brandon's educational, medical and governmental assistance followed. He attended an elementary school in Georgia with a program conducive to his former school in Louisiana.

(*See* **APPENDIX C**: 2008 Atlanta, Dekalb County, Georgia schools)

CHAPTER 4—
BRANDON MEETS DR. CHRIS

Age 5 years,
1 month

"[WGUN/Atlanta]
To Your Health
with Dr. Chris
Greene"

....
: *Reminder:*
:
: *Ask Dr. Chris about*
: *Brandon's pain*
: *threshold...*
....

DECEMBER 7, 2007 – BRANDON'S FIRST VISIT WITH DR. CHRIS

Once the family relocated to Georgia, Brandon's Uncle Charles emphasized nutrients and healthy eating which he attributed to Dr. Chris and **the most comprehensive and cutting-edge health show on radio [WGUN/Atlanta]—*To Your Health with Dr. Chris Greene***. Uncle Charles spoke of how eating healthy, by natural means, cured many ailments, such as colds, asthma, *etc.* Collectively, we thought Dr. Chris' theory made perfect sense. At least, it was something worth investigating. Soon after, an appointment was set for Brandon with Dr. Chris.[i]

Brandon Before Detox	
(5 years, 4 months)	
1.	Could not communicate (nonverbal)
2.	Could not process understanding
3.	Could not interact/play (isolated himself)
4.	Could not gesture
5.	Flapped his arms as though he were in flight
6.	Temper tantrums; cried constantly
7.	Resistant to change (cried long and uncontrollably)
8.	Banged his head on soft objects
9.	Stimmed
10.	Spun himself and objects
11.	Obsessed with object that spin
12.	Poor eating habits (ran after him)
13.	No social skills
14.	No emotions or personality
15.	Did not laugh or show expression
16.	No coordination
17.	No eye contact (blank starring)
18.	Not potty trained
19.	Constipated
20.	Would not sit still for more than a few seconds
21.	High tolerance/high threshold for pain (would not cry)
22.	Patted himself in the head or chest
23.	Parrot talked (seldom spoke—only repeated what he heard)
24.	Sensitive to sounds or loud noises
25.	Stimulated by texture and temperature
26.	Sucked on his articles of clothing (socks, shirts)
27.	Drooled constantly (would not swallow saliva)
28.	Would not follow directions
29.	Played unusually with objects
30.	Had to arrange things in a certain way
31.	Not aware of his surroundings
32.	Walked on his tip-toes

	Brandon After Detox **(5 years, 4 months to 5 years, 9 months)**
1.	Knows/says his name
2.	Knows how to spell his whole name
3.	Knows/says his date of birth
4.	Knows/says his age
5.	Knows/says his parents' names
6.	Knows/says his brother's name
7.	Recognizes and says, "Grandmommie"
8.	Recognizes and says, "Nanna" (has 2 Nannas)
9.	Knows and says the names of his immediate cousins (Zach & Zaria)
10.	Knows and says the names of his maternal grandparents (Papa and Joyce)
11.	Knows and says the names of his great-grandparents (MeMaw and Papa)
12.	Knows and calls his paternal grandfather (Pops)
13.	How to say night prayers ("Now I Lay Me Down to Sleep")
14.	Recites Philippians 4:13
15.	Knows/says grace … blesses his food
16.	Sings Donnie McClurkin's song, "We Fall Down"
17.	Sings his nursery rhymes ("Old McDonald", "Twinkle, Twinkle", etc.)
18.	Recites "The Pledge of Allegiance"
19.	Can dress himself (shirt, underwear, pants, socks and Velcro shoes (no tying))
20.	Can clean up after himself (toys, books, DVDs)
21.	Plays V-Smile educational video game(s)
22.	Spells over 200 words
23.	Potty trained (#1 and #2), flushes the toilet, washes and dries hands
24.	No bedwetting
25.	Bowls
26.	75% calmer
27.	Know/says days of the week
28.	Drinks lots of water
29.	Follows directions (allows us to direct and redirect him)
30.	Reads books (loves Dr. Seuss)
31.	Recognizes/knows numbers 1-100 and can spell most of them
32.	Recognizes colors
33.	Obedient in public (75% more)
34.	Allows us to brush his teeth (Aug. 4, 2008, he attempted to brush his own teeth)
35.	Brushes his hair (Aug. 3, 2008)
36.	Thought process 75% better
37.	Masters computer games ("*School Time*" Leap Frog, V-Tech Nitro *Notebook and Fisher Price Learning Letters Laptop*)
38.	Catches and throws balls
39.	Plays at *Chuck E. Cheese* (before, he cried and refused to enter)
40.	Shoots basketball
41.	Goes to the movies, restaurants, church, Sunday school and other activities (he is no longer disruptive)
42.	Responds to flash cards
43.	Throws kisses
44.	Gives great hugs (he initiates)
45.	Smiles and laughs aloud all the time
46.	Plays with objects with wheels correctly
47.	Loves "*Super Why*", "*Word World*", "*Barney*", "*Curious George*", "*Clifford*", "*Dragon Tales*", "*Wonder Pets*" and "*Wow, Wow, Wubbzy*"
48.	Loves Chris Brown and Ciera
49.	Voracious appetite (He says, "I love pizza, it's so hard to wait!" and "Juice please!")

	Brandon After Detox
	(5 years, 4 months to 5 years, 9 months) (CONTINUED)
50.	Eats and drinks healthy
51.	Drinks lots of water
52.	Has not been sick since March to present
53.	Fusses about change but allows change to happen
54.	Interacts with his brother
55.	Plays and interacts at play places
56.	Shows emotion
57.	Never constipated (goes two to three times a day)
58.	Knows his body parts (head, hair, eyes, nose, mouth, teeth, lips, tongue, cheeks, neck, shoulders, arms, elbows, stomach, back, legs, hands, fingers, thumb, pointer finger, legs, knees, feet, and toes) He says body parts during the "Tickle" game.
59.	Wears hats, glasses and headphones (Before, he did not tolerate having anything on his head, face or ears)
60.	Points and asks for objects
61.	Says whole sentences and puts words together in phrases
62.	Can walk his dog with a leash
63.	Can be kept by others outside of the immediately family
64.	Shows discipline and independence when he gets his own bananas, peels them and discards the banana peels into the trash receptacle.
65.	Retrieves his juice and/or water out of the refrigerator
66.	Loves DVD movies and responds to the movies
67.	Loves to take showers
68.	Loves to swim in wading pool (NO CHLORINE)
69.	Sleeps well

(Below is an excerpt from *Part II* of Dr. Chris Greene's **09/03/2008**, "Wake Up To Nutrition" Radio Show on *Autism (featuring Lynne George and Stuart Tomc[ii])).

LYNNE GEORGE: The pain threshold. That's the part that I'm worried about, but I noticed that it's getting better. Like Brandon—what causes that where Brandon, if he falls, it doesn't bother him?

DR. CHRIS: Well, I think part of that is remember how we were talking about yesterday with the vaccination concept is that it lowers certain levels of it—your body is not responding to inflammation as it is normally would. So, I think that that's part of it. And you have substance "P" level which typically will fluctuate widely. They can either go up or down which control and regulate pain throughout the body.

LYNNE GEORGE: Okay, so it does deal with the inflammation.

DR. CHRIS: Absolutely. So, what we're doing by giving him the nutritional supplements that we're doing, by giving him the infoceuticals, by understanding the probiotics that we're giving him, we're just—we're starting to reestablish

(CONTINUED - Excerpt from *Part II* of Dr. Chris Greene's **09/03/2008**, "Wake Up To Nutrition" Radio Show on *Autism (featuring Lynne George and Stuart Tomc)*).

that connection. So see, part of the problem, I think, with an autistic child is that there's the cell-to-cell communication is not there.

LYNNE GEORGE: Okay.

DR. CHRIS: You see. And, you do have inflammation, and it may be an overabundance of inflammation that can be creating problems and causing a lack of that cell-to-cell communication, so that when he puts his hand in a fire, he may not feel it initially.

LYNNE GEORGE: Right, it's like a delayed reaction.

DR. CHRIS: Delayed reaction, but that's because of the lack of the cell-to-cell communication. And now what you're seeing probably is that his pain threshold is starting to normalize.

LYNNE GEORGE: Right. Because he'll knock himself or fall down, and then it's like he'll think for a second—a few seconds—and all of a sudden, he'll come to me like, and you know, hold like whatever it is, and, you know—

DR. CHRIS: Be in pain.

LYNNE GEORGE: Exactly.

DR. CHRIS: And, that's a good sign. That's a real good sign. Lynne, wonderful. I know that you're going to be writing a book. We're going to be having you back on—just giving us updates on this. I appreciate you being with us.

LYNNE GEORGE: And, thank you, Dr. Chris, and thank you, Stuart.

STUART TOMC: Oh, my pleasure. And, I hope you wrote down the website there about the autism briefs.

LYNNE GEORGE: I sure did.

DR. CHRIS: Okay.

STUART TOMC: Because, you can contact them and share your story—

DR. CHRIS: That's going to be huge. We've got to get this word out; okay.

STUART TOMC: Because this goes out to all of the integrated physicians and all the practitioners that can make a difference.

LYNNE GEORGE: Oh, that's great.

STUART TOMC: And you **keep detailed notes of what Dr. Chris is putting him on**, and **we can track this and help other people break this terrible cycle**.

DR. CHRIS: That's what we want. Lynne, as always, thank you very much.

Dr. Chris: "We've got to get the word out; okay."

"Stuart Tomc: [K]eep detailed notes of what Dr. Chris is putting him on, and we can track this and help other people break this terrible cycle."

Brandon's first visit with Dr. Chris was December 7, 2007. Before any diagnosis, Dr. Chris took Brandon's hair sample to be analyzed. While waiting for the hair analysis' results, Brandon had three visits with Dr. Chris to prepare his body for detoxification. [Brandon's Nutri-Energetics Systems Scans© ("NES Scans")[iii] (Infoceutical Scan) were: 04/29/2008, 06/13/2008, 07/16/2008, and 08/28/2008.] (*See* **APPENDIX D**: Dr. Chris Greene (Appointments)).

(Below are excerpts from *Part I* of Dr. Chris Greene's **09/02/2008**, "Wake Up To Nutrition" Radio Show on *Autism* (*featuring Lynne George and Laurie Ledbetter*[iv])).

> *"I'm bringing in the grandmother [Lynne George] of one of my patients [Brandon] to tell her story in relationship to her grandson."*
> —*Dr. Chris Greene*

DR. CHRIS: I talk about education and being able to enlighten people in relationship to what's going on with themselves, their families, their bodies and how we're being affected environmentally and how we're being infected about the choices we make on a day-to-day basis. This is no exception today. As now, **I'm bringing in the grandmother [Lynne George] of one of my patients [Brandon] to tell her story in relationship to her grandson.** We'll get to her in just a moment. But, I want you to understand some things that I think is very important. Earlier this year, we had on CNN, and I normally don't like CNN—and I'll just tell you up front—but typically, I'd just go there for brief news bits—albeit bias news bits on—from Fox News of being bias to CNN being bias, but anyway, you look at it from this perspective. Byron Richards, who I respect a lot, who is a certified clinical nutritionist had written a great article on CNN helping to uncover the autism debacle that was blowing up in our government's face, and what we were talking about was on April 2nd, they spent a day bringing awareness of the problem of autism. They had Larry King's segment which included at the time Jenny McCarthy and Jim Carrey talking about her son who is autistic and her role of being able to bring him back from autism. And, make no mistake that it can be done. **Here's the problem that I have is when people come in, as a practitioner, what you want is a patient that is actually going to follow the advice that you give them, and many people come in with the expectation that there's going to be in one or two visits, that their life is going to be turned around.** You have to understand that a lot of the situations that we have today, and we're going to be talking about autism, in particular, but it doesn't really matter whether it's autism, whether it's Alzheimer's, whether it's any type of neurodegenerative disease, any type of autoimmune disease. All of these things have a common thread that you have to look at and really understand that it's going to take time to peel back layers that have been existing for a number of years. Now, when we look at—I'm going give you a brief history, and then we're going to get to our guest today....

> *"[A]s a practitioner, what you want is a patient that is actually going to follow the advice that you give them."*
> —*Dr. Chris Greene*

#   #   #

(Below are excerpts from *Part I* of Dr. Chris Greene's **09/02/2008**, "Wake Up To Nutrition" Radio Show on *Autism (featuring Lynne George and Laurie Ledbetter[v]*)).

> **DR. CHRIS:** One of the things that we look at—obviously, we've talked about hair analysis on this. One of the things that we have to look at is that many times we're measuring stress in the body, and people think most of the time, I'm just looking for minerals; right? I'm looking for heavy metals. That's an important component. There's no doubt. The other component though, is that we're looking at the endocrine system and how it's being stressed. We're looking at how the body is metabolizing sugars, the stress on the adrenal—as we talked with the hormones, the thyroid, the pancreas, protein utilization so that we know that the body is in a catabolic—tearing down phase, or is it in an anabolic phase, which is rebuilding? **Many times, especially with the spectrum of autism disorders that we're looking at, we're seeing that most of these children are in a catabolic state. In other words, their tissues are breaking down faster than they are repairing, and this was the case with Brandon, and what we saw is that his body was breaking down so much quicker than it was able to repair. And, that he had—he did, in fact, have heavy metal toxicity. So, we approached it from that standpoint... .**

(*See* **APPENDIX E**: 09/02/2008 Written Transcript of Dr. Chris Greene's "Wake Up To Nutrition" Radio Show (*featuring Lynne George and Laurie Ledbetter*)).

Below Dr. Natasha Campbell-McBride's take on Vaccinations (excerpt from "Gut and Psychology Syndrome," pages 59-61):

8. VACCINATIONS
DOES MMR CAUSE AUTISM?

The human mind is like an umbrella—
it functions best when open.
Walter Gropius, 1965

Talking about autism it is impossible to avoid the issue of the MMR vaccine and vaccination in general. In my practice I see some parents of autistic children who would link their child's disorder with the MMR (Measles, Mumps, and Rubella) vaccine where a majority cannot make this connection. An equal number of families connect their child's regression with DPT (Diphtheria, Pertussis and Tetanus) vaccination. Following research by Dr. Wakefield there has been a lot of publicity on this subject. The British government has put a lot of effort and money into convincing the public that the MMR vaccine is safe. While the MMR vaccine was in the limelight, other vaccines got questioned as well, due to the fact that many of them contain a preservative Thimerosal, a Mercury compound, and many other toxic and questionable substances. DPT vaccine containing Thimerosal has been banned in many countries. However, in Britain a fair amount old stock, containing Thimerosal, may still be injected into babies. Many vaccines are new and have not been tested long enough, yet apparently the number of complications from these vaccines is much higher then anybody would expect. On top of all this we have to remember that vaccines are commercial products made with profit in mind. Is it true that the £3 million, which the UK government recently spent on MMR promotion, was paid by the companies who have a commercial interest in this vaccine?

So, does MMR cause autism?

I do not believe that things are that simple. Here we have to look at vaccination as a whole.

Let us have a look at what is happening to children in our modern society. If you look around, how many healthy children do you see? Childhood asthma, eczema, diabetes, allergies, hay fever, digestive disorders, ADHD and autistic spectrum disorders have all gained epidemic proportions! The majority of siblings of autistic children have eczema, asthma or

> *"A compromised immune system is not going to react to environmental insults in the normal way!"*
>
> *—Dr. Natasha Campbell-McBride*

(CONTINUED - Excerpt from "Gut and Psychology Syndrome," by Dr. Natasha Campbell-McBride, pages 59-61.)

another one of those disorders. And though all these health problems appear to be different, they have one thing in common. A very big thing – a compromised immune system. A compromised immune system is not going to react to environmental insults in the normal way! Vaccination is a huge insult to the immune system. The manufacturers of vaccines produce them for children with normal immune systems which will react to these vaccines in a predictable way. However, in our modern society with our modern way of life, we are rapidly moving to a situation where a growing proportion of children do not have a normal immune system and will not produce an expected reaction to the vaccine. In some of these children vaccination, putting an enormous strain on an already compromised immune system, becomes that "last straw which breaks the camel's back" and brings on the beginning of autism, asthma, eczema, diabetes, etc. In other children, whose immune system is comprised to a lesser degree, vaccination will not start the disorder, but it will deepen the damage and move the child closer to it.

So while MMR and other vaccines may not be the direct cause of autism, in immune-compromised children they can do a lot of harm and in some children may well provide the trigger which starts the disorder.

Following all the scandals around vaccinations it is no surprise that a lot of people around the world express an opinion that we should abandon childhood vaccinations altogether. What these people forget is that before the vaccination era it was quite normal for every family to loose one, two, three and sometimes even more children to childhood infections, like measles, rubella, mumps and others. This is the natural selection law, which Mother Nature has imposed on all living creatures on Earth. No animal would have all of its young survive. In fact in many species most babies in the litter die with only the strongest surviving. This law of natural selection ensures that the planet is populated by the best and the fittest in each species. In our modern world we humans are not prepared to obey this law. No mother would allow her child to perish, when there are

"Vaccinations, which saved the lives of millions of children world-wide in the last century, are becoming dangerous thanks to changes in our life-styles."

—Dr. Natasha Campbell-McBride

(CONTINUED - Excerpt from "Gut and Psychology Syndrome," by Dr. Natasha Campbell-McBride, pages 59-61.)

ways to let the child live, despite the fact that this child may not be the best and the fittest she can produce. Childhood infections are one of the tools of natural selection. Children, who survive them, come out healthier with stronger immune systems, weak children are not supposed to survive them. Vaccinations are one of those ways we humans have invented to allow our weaklings to survive.

So, we cannot abandon vaccinations altogether unless we are prepared to obey the laws of Nature. We have to come up with a more rational approach to vaccinations. Vaccinations, which saved the lives of millions of children world-wide in the last century, are becoming dangerous thanks to changes in our life-styles. The number of immune-compromised children in developed countries is enormous and growing every day. It is time for the medical profession and governments to review their attitude to vaccinations. The rule to vaccinate everybody has to change!

In this book I propose the following procedure:

# # #

(Below is an excerpt from *Part II* of Dr. Chris Greene's **09/03/2008**, "Wake Up To Nutrition" Radio Show on *Autism (featuring Lynne George and Stuart Tomc)*).

DR. CHRIS: Alright. Welcome back everybody to another segment of to your health. I'm your host Dr. Chris Greene. Thanks for spending an hour of your time with us each and every day here Monday through Friday at WGUN Radio. You can listen also live to us at the internet at www.wgunradio.com, and as always, it's Wednesday. It's my good friend and colleague, Stuart Tomc that's going to be joining us this morning. I want to remind you also that you can call Dr. Chris' Natural Pharmacy. The number there is 770-979-5125. That's for appointments with myself and my good friend Dr. Dan Falorᵛ who is there. One of us is usually there Monday through Saturday for appointments. I'll be there through Saturday this week. I hope you guys are doing well. We had a very good talk yesterday with our good friend and Lynne George and Laurie Ledbetter. And, we were talking about Brandon, her grandson, his recovery or how he's really— we're seeing the reversing of autism with him, and

> *"We had a very good talk yesterday with our good friend and Lynne George and Laurie Ledbetter. And, we were talking about Brandon, her grandson, his recovery or how he's really—we're seeing the reversing of autism with him"*
>
> —Dr. Chris Greene

(CONTINUED - Excerpt from *Part II* of Dr. Chris Greene's **09/03/2008**, "Wake Up To Nutrition" Radio Show on *Autism* (*featuring Lynne George and Stuart Tomc*)).

we're going to talk a little bit about this morning. We've also got some things that we need to do with Stuart about some new studies on fish oil that has come out about heart failure. And I also want to talk about this issue with cholesterol and how low cholesterol actually increases cancer and death risks. This is a shot that's being heard quite prevalent now, and so, can we get cholesterol levels too low? Absolutely. What is cholesterol? It's a repair substance. That's what we have to remember. With that, let's go ahead and go to our good friend, Tony—Stuart Tomc—this morning. Good morning. How are you this morning?

(*See* **APPENDIX F**: 09/03/2008 Written Transcript of Dr. Chris Greene's "Wake Up To Nutrition" Radio Show (*featuring Lynne George and Stuart Tomc*)).

CHAPTER 5—
NUTRITION

> "An appropriate diet is an absolutely essential part of the treatment, but is definitely NOT the GFCF diet as we know it."
>
> —Dr. Natasha Campbell-McBride, author of "Gut and Psychology Syndrome" (page 73)

RECOMMENDED FOODS BY DR. NATASHA CAMPBELL-MCBRIDE[vi]

Almonds (including almond butter and oil)
Apples
Apricots, fresh or dried
Artichoke, French
Asiago cheese
Asparagus
Aubergine (eggplant)
Avocados, including avocado oil
Bananas (ripe only with brown spots on the skin)
Beans, dried white (navy, string beans and lima beans)
Beef, fresh or frozen
Beet or beetroot
Berries, all kinds
Black, white and red pepper (ground and pepper corns)
Black radish
Blue cheese
Bok Choy
Brazil nuts
Brick cheese
Brie cheese
Broccoli
Brussels sprouts
Butter
Cabbage
Camembert cheese
Canned fish in oil or water only
Capers
Carrots
Cashew nuts, fresh only
Cauliflower
Cayenne pepper
Celeriac
Celery
Cellulose in supplements
Cheddar cheese
Cherimoya (custard apple or sharifa)
Cherries
Chestnuts
Chicken, Fresh or frozen
Cinnamon
Citric Acid
Coconut, fresh or dried (shredded) without any additives
Coconut milk
Coconut oil
Coffee, weak and freshly made not instant
Collard greens
Colby cheese
Courgette

Coriander, fresh or dried
Cucumber
Dates, fresh or dried without any additives (not soaked in syrup)
Dill, fresh or dried
Duck, fresh or frozen
Edam cheese
Eggplant (aubergine)
Eggs, fresh
Filberts
Fish, fresh or frozen, canned in its juice or oil
Game, fresh or frozen
Garlic
Ghee, home-made
Gin, occasionally
Ginger root, fresh
Goose, fresh or frozen
Gorgonzola cheese
Gouda cheese
Grapefruit
Grapes
Havarti cheese
Hazelnuts
Herbal teas
Herbs, fresh or dried with additives
Honey, Natural
Juices freshly press from permitted fruit and vegetables
Kale
Kiwi fruit
Kumquats
Lamb, fresh or frozen
Lemons
Lentils
Lettuce, all kinds
Lima Beans (dried and fresh)
Limburger cheese
Limes
Mangoes,
Meats, fresh or frozen
Melons
Monterey (Jack) cheese
Mushrooms
Mustard seeds, pure powder and gourmet types without any non-allowed ingredients
Nectarines
Nut flour or ground nuts (usually ground blanched almonds)
Nutmeg
Nuts, all kinds freshly shelled, not roasted, salted or coated
Olive oil, virgin cold-pressed
Olives preserved without sugar or any other non-allowed ingredients
Onions
Oranges
Papayas

Parmesan cheese
Parsley
Peaches
Peanut butter, without additives
Peanuts, fresh or roasted in their shells
Pears
Peas, dried split and fresh green
Pecans
Peppers (green, yellow, read and orange)
Pheasant, fresh or frozen
Pickles, without sugar or any other non-allowed ingredients
Pigeon, fresh or frozen
Pineapples, fresh
Pork, fresh or frozen
Port du Salut Cheese
Poultry, fresh or frozen
Prunes, dried without any additives or in their own juice
Pumpkin
Quail, fresh or frozen
Raisins
Rhubarb
Roquefort cheese
Romano cheese
Satsumas
Scotch, occasionally
Shellfish, fresh or frozen
Spices, single and pure with any additives
Spinach
Squash (summer and winter)
Stilton cheese
String beans
Swiss cheese
Tangerines
Tea, weak freshly made, not instant
Tomato puree, pure without any additives apart from salt
Tomato juice, without any additives apart from salt
Tomatoes
Turkey, fresh or frozen
Turnips
Ugly fruit
Uncreamed cottage cheese (dry curd)
Vinegar (cider or white): make sure there is no allergy
Vodka, very occasionally
Walnuts
Watercress
Wine dry, red or white
Yoghurt, home-made
Zucchini

Dr. Natasha Campbell-McBride, MD. Gut and Psychology Syndrome. United Kingdom: Halstan Printing Group, Amersham, Buckinghamshire, Nov. 2007. (Recommended Foods. See pages 111-114).

FOODS TO AVOID BY DR. NATASHA CAMPBELL-MCBRIDE^		
Acesulphame	Chestnut flour	Millet
Acidophilus milk	Chevre cheese	Milk from any animal, say,
Agar-Agar	Chewing gum	rice canned coconut milk
Agave syrup	Chick peas	Milk, dried
Algae	Chickory root	Molasses
Aloe Vera	Chocolate	Mozzarella cheese
Amaranth	Chocolate	Mungbeans
Apple juice	Cocoa powder	Neufchatel cheese
Arrowroot	Coffee, instant and coffee	Nutra-sweet (aspartame)
Aspartame	substitutes	Nuts, salted, roasted and
Astragalus	Cooking oils	coated
Baked Beans	Cordials	Oats
Baker's yeast	Corn	Okra
Baking power and raising agents	Cornstarch	Parsnips
of all kinds	Corn syrup	Pasta, of any kind
Balsamic vinegar	Cottage cheese	Pectin
Barley	Cottonseed	Postum
Bean flour and sprouts	Couscous	Potato white
Bee pollen	Cream	Potato sweet
Beer	Cream of Tartar	Primost cheese
Bhindi or okra	Cream cheese	Quinoa
Bicarbonate of soda	Dextrose	Rice
Bitter Gourd	Drinks, soft	Ricotta cheese
Black eye beans	Faba beans	Rye
Bologna	Feta cheese	Saccharin
Bouillon cubes or granules	Fish, preserved, smoked, salted,	Sago
Brandy	breaded and canned with sauces	Sausages, commercially
Buckwheat	Flour, made out of grains	available
Bulgur	FOS (fructooligosaccharides)	Seaweed
Burdock root	Fructose	Semolina
Butter beans	Fruit, canned or preserved	Sherry
Buttermilk	Garbanzo beans	Soda soft drinks
Canellini beans	Gjetost cheese	Sour cream commercial
Canned vegetables and fruit	Grains, all	Soy
Carob	Gruyere cheese	Spelt
Carrageenan	Ham	Starch
Cellulose gum	Hotdogs	Sugar or sucrose of
Cereals, including all breakfast	Ice-cream, commercial	any kind
cereals	Jams	Tapioca
Cheeses, processed and cheese	Jellies	Tea, instant
spreads	Jerusalem artichoke	Tricale
	Ketchup, commercially available	Turkey loaf
	Lactose	Vegetables, canned or
	Liqueurs	preserved
	Margarines and butter replacements	Wheat
	Meats, process, preserved,	Wheat germ
	smoked and salted	Whey, powder or liquid
		Yams
		Yoghurt, commercial

Dr. Natasha Campbell-McBride, MD. Gut and Psychology Syndrome.
United Kingdom: Halstan Printing Group, Amersham, Buckinghamshire, Nov. 2007.
(Foods to Avoid. See pages 115-118).

I often prayed that Brandon would be able to deviate from his current diet without any setbacks. I was fortunate to have a discussion with experts:

(Below is an excerpt from *Part I* of Dr. Chris Greene's **09/02/2008**, "Wake Up To Nutrition" Radio Show on *Autism (featuring Lynne George and Laurie Ledbetter)*).

LYNNE GEORGE: Yes, like if he would sneak a piece of bread or something like that, you can notice the reversion, because he doesn't pay attention. He's not as directive. He can't—
DR. CHRIS: Right.
LYNNE GEORGE: —you know—he's just out of control a little bit, but then, once he gets his nutrients back in him, he's fine. He can—it takes a couple of hours if he sneaks something, and so, once he's on this healthy regime, he has to stick with it the rest of his life.

Laurie Ledbetter (Dr. Natasha Campbell-McBride's representative/distributor) says:

LAURIE LEDBETTER: —for up to eight weeks, sometimes particularly autistic children, it can take up to two years. So, she [Dr. Natasha Campbell-McBride] does say that you can get you can get to a point where the gut can be healed to the point where you do not have to follow Brandon around. It takes time like you said, Dr. Chris. This is not going to be healed over night. You cannot do it. It's not going to absorb in a couple of months. It is going to take time to repair the damage, but she has found not only with her patients but with her own son that she does not have to following around anymore, that she can go on vacation, and as he eats some of these foods that would normally cause this horrible reaction, that he can eat it and it does not cause the reaction, then they go back home and get back on the diet. So, there is a sort of some hope in there from what she see is that it can be healed to a very large degree, not that you can go back to the old way of healing and eating that caused this situation in the beginning, but that you can venture into that world of eating every once in a while and come out of it and not see the reactions that you see. So, I would say just hang in there and keep working with those probiotics, because it just takes a while to heal the gut.

(Below are excerpts from "Gut and Psychology Syndrome," by Dr. Natasha Campbell-McBride, page 69.)

A human body has an incredible ability to heal itself, given the right help. It is particularly true for children.

\#   \#   \#

> *"[S]he [Dr. Natasha Campbell-McBride] does say that you can get to a point where the gut can be healed..."*
>
> *—Laurie Ledbetter, Representative/Distributor for Dr. Natasha Campbell-McBride, author of "Gut and Psychology Syndrome" (09/02/08 Dr. Chris Greene's "Wake Up To Nutrition" Radio Show regarding "Autism" (featuring Lynne George and Laurie Ledbetter))*

> *"[D]etoxification and life-style changes"*

The Nutritional Programme for Gut and Psychology Syndrome

1. Diet.
2. Supplementation.
3. Detoxification and life-style changes.

# # #

THE REMAINDER OF THIS PAGE
IS INTENTIONALLY BLANK.

CHAPTER 6—
REVERSING BRANDON'S AUTISM "NATURALLY"

> *"[N]utrients promote frequent restroom visits."*

> *"[H]is breath smelled like week-old garbage."*

> *"If you guys could just hang in there, everything is going to be alright."*

REVERSING BRANDON'S AUTISM...

While Brandon attends school, he is not administered his nutrients until he returns home. These nutrients promote frequent restroom visits. However, non-school days, Brandon is administered his nutrients first thing in the morning.

BRANDON'S DETOXIFICATION – APRIL 2008

Brandon's detox symptoms surfaced the second week of April 2008. At that time, his breath smelled like week-old garbage. He was congested. His lymph nodes were swollen. He could not swallow. He moved as though his neck were stiff. Brandon was very lethargic for **four days**. He had diarrhea 24/7. He expelled so much liquid that it ran through his *Pull-ups* and onto his clothing. When we called Dr. Chris, he explained and reassured us regarding the stages of Brandon's detox process. Brandon's clothing was soiled and changed nearly 15 times a day. He slept a lot and was enormously congested to the point that he could only breathe through his mouth. We gave him juices which he sipped very little, and he ate bits of bananas. Brandon was already slender which later turned to skinny. By **day five**, the swelling in his neck reduced. He drank and ate more fresh juices and bananas. By **day seven**, a rash appeared over his entire body that looked similar to chill bumps. Again, we consulted with Dr. Chris who assured us with these words: "If you guys could just hang in there, everything is going to be alright." The rash lasted two days. To our relief, on the **eighth** morning, the rash disappeared. Brandon's skin was so beautiful—it was glowing. And first the time in Brandon's life, he had an appetite. He started eating voraciously.

I am truly convinced that if it were not for God, prayer, our family's concern for Brandon, and the combination of Drs. "Chris" and Campbell-McBride, the success of reversing Brandon's autism "naturally" would not be possible.

Dr. Chris was instrumental in preparing Brandon's gut through nutrients and homeopathic supplements. (*See also* **APPENDIX D**: Dr. Chris Greene (Appointments)).

(Below is an excerpt from *Part I* of Dr. Chris Greene's **09/02/2008**, "Wake Up To Nutrition" Radio Show on *Autism (featuring Lynne George and Laurie Ledbetter)*).

In other words, their **tissues are breaking down faster than they are repairing, and this was the case with Brandon**, and what we saw is that his body was breaking down so much quicker than it was able to repair.

Dr. Natasha Campbell-McBride gave our family the "perfect" reference tool to assist us in reversing Brandon's autism naturally through nutrition. Below, I would like to share an excerpt from GAPS:

("Gut and Psychology Syndrome," by Dr. Natasha Campbell-McBride, pages 74-75.)

> GAPS children and adults are very toxic. Tests show that they store heavy metals, petrochemicals and other toxic substances in the tissues of their bodies sometimes in frightening amounts. Many of these toxins are probably responsible for various physical and mental symptoms in GAPS patients. For example, there are great similarities in the clinical picture of acute poisoning with mercury, lead and other toxins, found in these patients, and the clinical picture of autism and psychosis. Based on these findings **recently there has been a lot of attention to heavy metal chelation in autism**, the purpose of which is to take heavy metals out of the body. Anybody familiar with chelation knows that this process always involves the child going through a detox period, when autistic symptoms get worse and a lot of unpleasant new physical symptoms occur. Why? Because chelation drugs wash out stored heavy metals from the tissues into the blood to be taken out of the body. This "cleaning up" process causes symptoms, often quite severe.
>
> There is no doubt that detoxification or elimination of toxic substance has to be an integral part of the treatment for GAPS patients. Natural phenols found in foods are the Nature's way of eliminating toxins from the body on a daily basis. So, the last thing we should do is to cut them out of the diet. Of course, in the process of "cleaning up" they will cause the "detox reaction". Most phenols in the foods will not cause a severe reaction (unless the patient has true allergy to a particular food). The child or adult may experience worsening of behavior and sleep, more self-stimulation, more hyperactivity and mood swings. This period is temporary and most patients survive it very well. As the body starts to detoxify, the negative reaction usually goes away. If your GAPS child or adult is particularly sensitive to some food, cut it out of the diet for 4-6 weeks and then introduce it slowly starting from tiny amounts and gradually increasing them. This way you can keep the detox reaction under control. The important thing is to make sure that the person has not got a true allergy to that particular food, which can be tested for in most medical facilities.

#   #   #

"[T]he "perfect" reference tool to assist us in reversing Brandon's autism naturally... GAPS"

"Natural phenols found in foods are the Nature's way of eliminating toxins from the body on a daily basis."
—Dr. Natasha Campbell-McBride

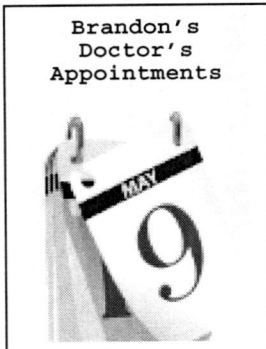

We tailored Drs. Chris' and Campbell-McBride's methods *together* which made great strides in unlocking Brandon's window of autism.

Brandon's Doctor's Appointments

Brandon's
Doctor's
Appointments

- 12/07/2007 – First visit with Dr. Chris Greene; Hair Analysis and Nutrients
- 12/14/2007 – Nutrients given
- 02/08/2008 – Nutrients given
- 03/20/2008 – Nutrients given; purchased "Gut and Psychology" from Dr. Chris
- 04/29/2008 – NES Scan© and Nutrients
- 06/13/2008 – NES Scan© and Nutrients
- 07/16/2008 – NES Scan© and Nutrients
- 08/28/2008 – NES Scan© and Nutrients
- TO DATE: Brandon visits Dr. Chris every four weeks

Date: 12/07/2007
Narrative: Brandon's first visit with Dr. Chris, accompanied by his Grandmommie and Mother. (*See also* **APPENDIX D**: Dr. Chris Green (Appointments)).

Physical complaints:
Brandon will only eat finger foods
Brandon will not eat from a spoon of fork
Brandon will only take his vitamins in liquid form and dispense into his sippy cup or juice cup
Concerned about Brandon's nutrition

Date: 12/07/2007 *(CONTINUED)*
Narrative: Dr. Chris gave Brandon the basic visit and ordered a hair analysis. The hair analysis would take a few months to come in.
Products: (started by Dr. Chris)
Malvin   (5 drops, 3x/day)
Dopamine   (5 drops, 3x/day)
Taurine   (5 drops, 3x/day)
Butter oil   (1/2 tsp, 2x/day)
Cod liver oil - High DHA   (1 tsp, 2x/day)
Follow-up next week

BRANDON'S NATURAL DETOXIFICATION BEGINS

Date: 12/14/2007
Narrative: Brandon's second visit with Dr. Chris
Dr. Chris gave special instructions to follow the gluten-free, casein-free diet. He introduced Bio-Kult to Brandon's product schedule
week 1   1@ breakfast, 1@dinner
week 2   2@ breakfast, 2@dinner
week 3   3@ breakfast, 3@dinner
week 4-11   3@ breakfast, 3@dinner
week 12-15   2@ breakfast, 2@dinner
maintenance   1@ breakfast, 1@dinner
acetylaldehyde   (5 drops, 3x/day)
All else the same
Follow-up 3 weeks

Date: 02/08/2008

Narrative: Brandon's third visit with Dr. Chris. Dr Chris suggested that we read Dr. Natasha Campbell-McBride's book "Gut and Psychology Syndrome, Natural Treatment for Autism, Dyspraxia, A.D.D., Dyslexia, A.D.H.D, Depression and Schizophrenia". Dr. Campbell-McBride, (MMedSci(neurology), MMedSci(nutrition).

Products:

Flush-eez	(2 squirts, 3x/day)
Bio-Kult (resumed)	
Adrenal support	(8 drops, 3x/day)
Metox	(5 drops, 3x/day)
Camu powder	(1/2 tsp, 3x/day)
All else the same	

Follow-up 4 weeks

Bio-Kult, an Advanced Probiotic Formula containing fourteen strains of beneficial bacteria. It is formulated specifically to help maintain a healthy gut flora, resulting in improved function of the Digestive and Immune Systems.

"Gut and Psychology Syndrome" (GAP syndrome or GAPS) reveals the true connection between nutrition and brain function. Written by a neurologist and practicing nutritionist it is a "no holds barred" investigation into the real facts behind why today's generation of children have the highest incidence of learning disabilities and behavioral disorders ever.

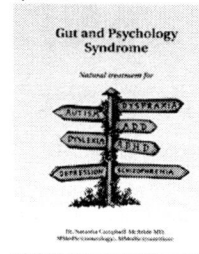

Through Dr. Chris'[vii] recommendation, Brandon's Mother and Grandmommie purchased and read "Gut and Psychology Syndrome" by Dr. Natasha Campbell-McBride. Grandmommie was intrigued to discover that Dr. Natasha was the mother of an autistic child. Grandmommie enthusiastically shared with the family various points of interest in "Gut and Psychology" that related to Brandon. In layman's terms, these points equipped her with essential, fundamental tools, such as *Recommended Foods*, *Foods to Avoid*, recipes, the use of proper utensils/appliances, and so much more.

I purchased my very own copy of "Gut and Psychology". I felt empowered. Throughout Dr. Campbell-McBride's book, it was as though she personally spoke to me—informing and explaining the scope of autism—the "when", "where", "why" and "how" the gut was connected to the brain. To date, our family owns several copies of this wonderful book. It is basically our reference tool to "*reversing Brandon's autism naturally*".

"The fact that this kind of GFCF [Gluten Free Casein Free] diet gained such a world-wide acceptance as the diet for autism is very unfortunate, because it addresses only a small part of the whole picture of autism: **The gluteomorphins and casomorphins.***"*

"An appropriate diet is an absolutely essential part of the treatment. But it is definitely not the GFCF diet as we know it."
—*Dr. Natasha Campbell-McBride*

(Below are excerpts from "Gut and Psychology Syndrome," by Dr. Natasha Campbell-McBride, pages 72-73 and 83.)

The fact that this kind of **GFCF [Gluten Free Casein Free]** diet gained such a world-wide acceptance as the diet for autism is very unfortunate, because it addresses only a small part of the whole picture of autism: The gluteomorphins and casomorphins. As it always happens a lot of commercial companies jumped on the bandwagon, ready to supply GFCF pre-prepared foods full of sugar, process carbohydrates, denature and altered facts and proteins and many other substances, which autistic children must not have. Every publication on autism is full of advertisements for these foods, lulling the parents into a sense of false security: If it is GFCF it must be fine for my autistic child. Books are written full of recipes based on the processed carbohydrates, sugar, altered fats and proteins. Web-sites and internet chat groups have been set up exchanging the same kind of recipe....

This is just another example of what already happened many times in our human history: Scientific data has been used the wrong way. There is no doubt, that gluten and casein are better out of the diet of an autistic child. But these two substances are by no means the one and only decisive key to autism, schizophrenia and other GAPS conditions. The core issue, which we have to deal with, is the unhealthy gut ruled by abnormal microbes. An appropriate diet is an absolutely essential part of the treatment. But it is definitely not the GFCF diet as we know it.

# # #

"No processed foods, please!"

# # #

("Gut and Psychology Syndrome", page 83.)

Date: 03/20/2008
Narrative: Brandon's 4th visit with Dr. Chris
Product:
Chemtox   (8 drops, 3x/day)
Health Bac   (1 teaspoon/day)
ES8   (6 drops, 2x/day in water)
Blocked left ear chemicals
Follow-up April 29 @ 5p (with associate Dr. Dan. NES Scan© next visit)

Detox Period: April 6 through April 13
(8 days)

APRIL 6	DR. CHRIS GREENE'S and DR. NATASHA CAMPBELL-McBRIDE'S COMBINED NATURAL DETOXIFICATION METHODS BEGAN.
APRIL 12	RASH APPEARED ON HIS ENTIRE BODY. (SIMILAR TO GOOSE BUMPS)
APRIL 13	RASH REMAINED. IMPURITIES MANIFESTED.
APRIL 14	RASH DISAPPEARED. BRANDON SPEAKS FOR THE VERY FIRST TIME: "What are you doing Nanna?"
APRIL 17	BRANDON RETURNED TO SCHOOL.

Dr. Chris, HELP!

Date: 04/29/2008
Narrative: Brandon's 5th visit (his 1st NES Scan©)
(These instructions are at the top of each Nutri-Energetics Infoceutical Protocol)
Instructions:
Take Infoceuticals in the order listed below starting with "1"
Take Infoceuticals separately. Do not mix unless directed to do so.
Place indicate number of drops in a glass of purified water and drink immediately
Leave at least 10 minutes between taking each infoceutical.

NOTE: This statement is on the bottom of each Nutri-Energetics Infoceutical Protocol

"During the first 7-10 days when starting on infoceuticals, you may have a detox reaction (this is not a side effect as there are not biochemical substances in these products). Detox means that the body is attempting to eliminate toxins. You may notice changes in color or smell in urine, bowel movements, minor irritability, sores or bumps under the skin or in the mouth or tiredness. Stronger detox reactions include, nausea, headaches and interrupted sleep. If this happens, stop taking preparations for 3 days then resume taking them at a dosage reduced by 50%. If you have any questions, please call. These energetic preparations will not interfere with supplements, prescriptions drugs or herbal preparations."

Date: 04/29/2008
Narrative: Dr. Chris gives another Nutri-Energetics Infoceutical Protocol Schedule for a month, along with the dosage for that month.
Products:
PL, ED6, ED10, ED13, ES8

MAY 25	BRANDON ARRIVED AT HIS MAMMAW'S AND PAWPAW'S IN FLORIDA.
MAY 31	BRANDON GAVE NANNA A BIRTHDAY PRESENT WHEN HE SPELLED OVER 100 WORDS WITH HIS ALPHABET BLOCKS.

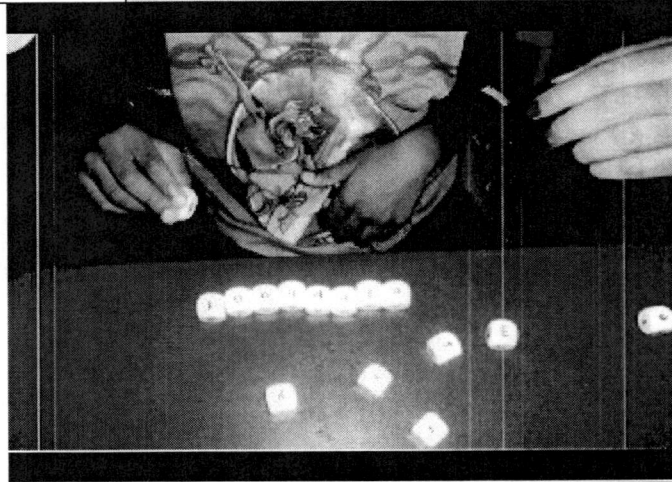

SURPRISE!

NANNA

Brandon spelled the word "elephant".

Social Activities: May 26 through June 6

- Played on slip-n-slide with brother and friend
- Played with friends at Burger King's play area
- Bowled with family friends
- Went to Disney World/Universal Studios
- Waded and played in pool (non-chlorinated)
- Watched movie ("Kung-Fu Panda")
- Watched DVDs
- Played with computer games
- Spelled with alphabet block
- Played basketball at Chuck E. Cheese

NOTE: A special lunch is packed for Brandon on any outings.

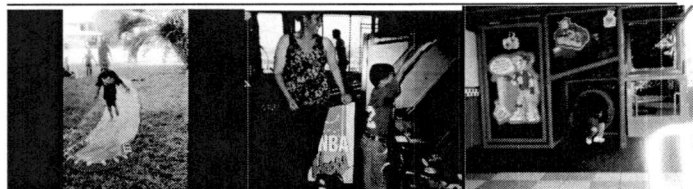

Brandon at play: Slip-n-Slide, Chuck E. Cheese and Indoor Play Center at Burger King

Date:　06/13/2008
Narrative: Brandon's 6th visit with Dr. Chris (2nd NES Scan©).
Dr. Chris gave a Nutri-Energetics Infoceutial Protocol schedule for a month, along with the dosage.
Products:
ED9, EI8, EI10, ES8, ESR
Recommendations: #4&5 Stay on
Next visit ETO & ET8
Follow-up 4 weeks. Next appointment July 16 @ 4:45p

JUNE 7	LYNNE RETURNED TO LOUISIANA.
JUNE 9 THRU JULY 18	BRANDON ATTENDED EXTENDED SCHOOL YEAR ("ESY") AGE 5, 7 MONTHS: BRANDON WAS NOT POTTY TRAINED.

Date:　07/16/2008
Narrative: Brandon's 7th visit with Dr. Chris (3rd NES Scan©).
Dr. Chris gave a Nutri-Energetics Infoceutical Protocol schedule for a month, along with the dosage.
Products:
ED3, ED8, EI7, ET4, ES5,
ES8 and ESR same
Recommendations: First time to speak since beginning gave name/birthday.
Next appointment 30 days (August 20 @ 11:00)

JUNE 25	LYNNE RETURNED TO GEORGIA.
JULY 20	BRANDON STARTED POTTY TRAINING.

Education: June 25 through July 20

Brandon learned to:

Recognize numbers 1-100
Say his full name
Say his birthday
Say his parents' names
Say his brother's name
Blow kisses
Recite bible verses (Phil. 4:13)
Do simple addition
Identify body parts
Play ball with his brother
Walk his dog
Respond correctly
Sing songs

Brush his teeth
Brush his hair
Put waste in receptacles
Use potty independently
Dress himself
Say Grace
Make polite requests
Read
Recite months of the year
Recite days of the week
Spell his name
　Etc.

Date: 08/28/2008
Narrative: Brandon's 8th visit with Dr. Chris (4th NES Scan©).
Dr. Chris gave a Nutri-Energetics Infoceutical Protocol schedule for a month, along with the dosage.
Products:
ED 4, ED6, EI9, ET7, ES10,
ESR and ES8 same
Recommendations: Cod liver & Butter oil 1 tablespoon each
Next appointment: 2 & 4 week. September 16 @ 5:00 and October 7 @ 5:30

> **Brandon continues to see Dr. Chris every four weeks.**

> **Brandon has not been sick since his detox. "Thank you, Jesus!" However, other family members within the same household have not been so fortunate. Other members have suffered with colds, allergies, viruses, etc.**

(Below is an excerpt from *Part I* of Dr. Chris Greene's **09/02/2008**, "Wake Up To Nutrition" Radio Show on *Autism (featuring Lynne George and Laurie Ledbetter)*).

DR. CHRIS: Lynne, you brought out a great point. If we had been following this from the time that you first noticed it, how much further would Brandon be? I guess that was really your question; wasn't it?
LYNNE GEORGE: Yes, because I'm amazed that, you know, it's only been going on the fifth month. You know, like I say, he doing something new every time, but I was asking you if we would have started it like when we noticed it like after 17 months, when he was diagnosed and evaluated—
DR. CHRIS: Right.
LYNNE GEORGE: —with autism, you know, what kind of—
DR. CHRIS: Results would you have seen.
LYNNE GEORGE: —yes, results.
DR. CHRIS: The other thing that I think that you were frustrated about is the lack of people doing this and recognizing that these problems in the first place.
LYNNE GEORGE: Yes.
DR. CHRIS: I mean, was that not one of the key factors here that there was an—
LYNNE GEORGE: Yes.
DR. CHRIS: —area of frustration?
LYNNE GEORGE: I was frustrated, because, you know, attorneys are going to seek restitution. That's fine. You know, and doctors are going to try find a cure, but what's going on now with the person who has autism now. We have to have to help them now. You know, so I just looked at it and said, I have to help my grandson some kind of way, and I feel God has made me in a situation where I have a back debilitation, and I'm there all the time—

> *"Lynne, you brought out a great point. If we had been following this from the time that you first noticed it [autism], how much further would Brandon be?"*

DR. CHRIS: Right.
LYNNE GEORGE: —to be with him, and they have to have that. They have to have—everything is a culmination of everything.

Since December 14, 2007, Brandon's mainstay of nutrients (each morning and evening), in addition to the above:

Bio-Kult	(1 capsule)
Camu Camu	(1/2 teaspoon)
Artic Cod Liver Oil	(1 teaspoon)
Flush-EZ	(1 squirt)

Summary of Products/Services
from December 12, 2007
to August 28, 2008

Acetylaldehyde
Adrenal support
Artic Cod liver oil
Bio-Kult
Butter oil
Camu Powder
Dopamine
ED3
ED4
ED6
ED8
ED9
ED10
ED13
EI7
EI8
EI9
EI10
ES5
ES8
ES10
ESR
ET4
Flush-eez
Hair Analysis
Health Bac
Malvin
Metox
PL
Taurine

Dr. Chris' Natural Pharmacy
(Brandon's Monthly Expenses)

$40.00	Dr. Chris' Fee (per visit)
$300.00	Cost of Nutrients and Whole Food Supplements
$340.00	

CHAPTER 7—
BRANDON'S
RECIPES

After the **eighth day of detox**, Brandon ate healthier foods: pizza (yes, pizza!)—but <u>not</u> the traditional pizza; a minimum of seven bananas each day; breakfast juices; and lemonade—all made from natural ingredients. Nutrients are added in every glass of Brandon's breakfast juice, lemonade and water. We were able to create Brandon's Pizza, Juice and Lemonade recipes from Dr. Natasha Campbell-McBride's "Gut and Psychology": *Recommended Foods* and *Foods to Avoid* lists.

Also, Brandon's activities increased tremendously. He was a pure boy—active and mischievous with a budding personality. His eyes gleamed. We were amazed at his voracious appetite. We had never seen Brandon eat like that before. And, he seemed to enjoy eating immensely.

BRANDON'S DAILY EATING AND DRINKING SCHEDULE	
Time	*Foods*
6:45	Breakfast juice and a banana
8:00	Banana and water
10:00	Pizza and lemonade
11:00	Banana and water
12:00	Banana and water
2:00	Pizza and breakfast juice
4:00	Banana and water
5:00	Banana and water
6:00	Pizza and lemonade
7:00	Banana and water
8:00	Banana and water

In a course of a day, Brandon may consume: Seven 10-ounce glass of purified water, with a teaspoon of honey[1] in each glass of water to ensure that he gets his nutrients and a minimum of seven ripe bananas.

---

[1] Honey is optional.

Brandon's Consumption of Pizza, Breakfast Juice and Lemonade

Within a four-day period, Brandon may consume 6 oranges, 1 pint of strawberries, 2 apples, 3 limes, 3 lemons, a handful of carrots, ½ bell pepper, ½ beet root, 2 whole tomatoes, 2 handfuls of baby spring mix, 3 cloves of garlic, 2 cups of almonds, 12 slices of pepperoni, 1 breast of chicken, 3 large fresh eggs, 1 pound of cheese, 3 teaspoons of butter or ghee, and 2 cups of honey, 1 teaspoon of sea salt, 1 teaspoon of pepper, and ½ gallon of purified water (for lemonade).

Within five days, Brandon may also consume 350 ounces of water and 35 bananas.

The nutrients contained in these foods give Brandon a voracious appetite. His new desire and willingness to eat make us conscientious to eat healthier foods. Remarkably, the foods satisfy his appetite, and he does not crave junk food. Amazingly so, Brandon independently goes to the refrigerator and retrieves his prepared drinks. We learned replenish his juice and water stock. Brandon also retrieves, peels, eats and discards his bananas.

Before leaving for school, Brandon has his first breakfast juice and banana. He consumes 2 to 3 bananas, a slice of pizza (warmed in oven then stored in plastic container), 10 ounces of water and 10 ounces of lemonade. When he returns home, his afternoon food schedule begins with more pizza and breakfast juice.

When traveling, Brandon's food items are packed to prepare and maintain his eating schedule. We continue to introduce new food items to Brandon's diet items from Dr. Natasha Campbell-McBride's Recommended Foods list.

The cost of Brandon's monthly food is below:

Brandon's Diet	
(Brandon's Monthly Expenses)	
$250.00	Food Expenses (Pizza, Lemonade,
$250.00	Breakfast Juice, Bananas and Water)

BON APPETITE!

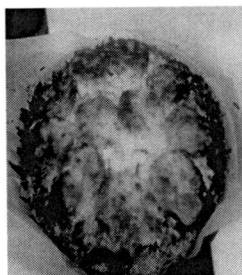

Actual picture of
Brandon's Pizza

"SAY CHEESE!"

(Cheese from the
"GAPS"
*Recommended
Foods* list):

- Asiago
- Blue Cheese
- Brick
- Brie
- Colby
- Gorgonzola
- Gouda
- Havarti
- Monterey Jack
- Limberger
- Muenster
- Parmesan
- Port du Salut
- Roquefort
- Romano
- Stilton
- Swiss

BRANDON'S PIZZA

Utensils:
Parchment paper
Grater
Wooden spoon
Pizza pan
Sauce pan
Knife
Blender
Bowl
Chopping board
A small glass pot and a small glass dish
Oven (no microwaving)

Ingredients for the crust of the pizza:
2 cups of almonds
2 large fresh whole eggs (or 3 small fresh whole eggs)
1 teaspoon butter (or ghee)
½ teaspoon of sea salt
½ teaspoon of ground pepper
Ingredients needed for the meat:
½ teaspoon of sea salt
½ teaspoon of ground pepper
1 or 2 pieces of meat from "GAPS'" *Recommended Foods'* list
12 slices of pepperoni
Ingredients needed for the pizza sauce:
½ bell pepper (red, yellow or green)
3 cloves garlic (chopped/minced)
1 tablespoon of butter (or ghee)
2 fresh large whole tomatoes (or 4 fresh Roma tomatoes) **(Pureed)**
1 tablespoons of honey (optional as sweetener)
½ teaspoon of sea salt
½ teaspoon of ground pepper
½ cup of shredded carrots
Ingredients for the vegetables:
2 handfuls of baby spring mix
Cheese:
1 pound of grated cheese from the "GAPS'" *Recommended Foods* list

Step 1 (Meat): Season meat with sea salt and ground pepper and bake/cook in glass dish until brown. (Once cooled, chop meat.) While meat is cooking...
Step 2 (Crust): Grind almonds to a powdery consistency. Pour powered almonds into bowl.
Add butter (or ghee), eggs, sea salt and ground pepper to powdery almonds. Mix until pasty consistency. (Note: If spreading the almond paste by hand, moisten hands first with water.) Cover pizza pan with parchment paper. Flatten and cover parchment pan with almond paste. Bake for 10 minutes at 350 degrees.
Step 3: Add butter, bell pepper and garlic to glass pot (sauté).
Add puree to mixture and simmer for 15 minutes on medium heat.
Step 4: Rinse two handfuls of spring mix. Pat dry. Then chop spring mix until fine.
Step 5: Spreading generous layers: 1) Spread pizza sauce over crust; 2) then spring mix; 3) then meat (not pepperoni); 4) then pepperoni; and 5) finally cheese.
Step 6: Bake for 30 minutes at 350 degrees. Let cool before serving.
(Pizza recipe was created by Ms. Shirley Brown *aka* "Brandon's Grandmommie".)

BRANDON'S BREAKFAST JUICE

<u>Utensils</u>:
Juicer
Blender

<u>Ingredients</u>:
6 oranges
2 apples
½ pint of strawberries
1 fresh egg
1 cup of honey
½ cup of ice

<u>Directions</u>:
<u>Step 1</u>: Juice the oranges, apples and strawberries
<u>Step 2</u>: Place the juice mixture in blender
<u>Step 3</u>:   Add egg, honey and ice
Blend and refrigerate

BRANDON'S LEMONADE

<u>Utensils</u>:
Juicer
Blender

<u>Ingredients</u>:
3 lemons
2 limes
½ beet root
1 cup of honey
2 cups of ice
1 gallon of purified water

<u>Directions</u>:
<u>Step 1</u>: Juice beet root (Place ½ of beet root juice aside)
<u>Step 2</u>: Juice lemons and limes (Place ½ of lemon and lime juice aside)
<u>Step 3</u>: Blend ½ of the beet root juice; ½ of the lemon/lime juice; honey and ice and fill with purified water to top portion of blender
<u>Step 4</u>: Pour into a container
Repeat steps 3 and 4 with remaining mixture
Place in a container and refrigerate.

(Brandon's Lemonade and Brandon's Breakfast Juice recipes were created by Mr. Charles Brown *aka* "Brandon's Uncle Charles".)

CHAPTER 8—
"GUT AND PSYCHOLOGY"— DR. NATASHA CAMPBELL-MCBRIDE

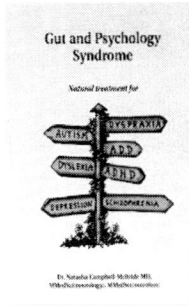

Gut and Psychology Syndrome

Natural treatment for

AUTISM, DYSPRAXIA, A.D.D., DYSLEXIA, A.D.H.D., DEPRESSION, SCHIZOPHRENIA

Dr. Natasha Campbell-McBride MD, MMedSci(neurology), MMedSci(nutrition)

"You can't fix the problem if you don't know about the source."

I strongly recommend "Gut and Psychology Syndrome"—Natural Treatment for **Autism,** **Dyspraxia, A.D.D., Dyslexia, A.D.H.D, Depression and Schizophrenia**, by Dr. Natasha Campbell-McBride MD, MMedSci(neurology), MMedSci(nutrition) ("GAPS").

I attribute Dr. Campbell-McBride's book to be an integral part to Brandon's successful reversal of autism naturally.

The book opened our eyes to understand, in layman's terms, how the gut and the brain are connected. I understand why Ms. Shirley (Brandon's Grandmommie) raved with excitement. She shared excerpts of the book which made me hunger for more knowledge on autism and how we should commit ourselves to treat Brandon's autism naturally. Grandmommie said, "You can't fix the problem if you don't know about the source." That is what "Gut and Psychology" explains and reveals in plain and simple terms.

"Gut and Psychology" has become our reference tool to effectively aid us in combating Brandon's autism naturally. Brandon has a diligent, loving and supportive team, because it does takes a village to raise a child, especially one with autism. And, we have equipped our village with several copies of Dr. Campbell-McBride's book. "Gut and Psychology" empowered our family to be on one accord. This book has allowed us to make great strides in reversing Brandon's autism naturally.

The reason why I believe this book is such a powerful reference tool is that the Dr. Natasha Campbell-McBride is not only a doctor but she is a mother who used natural treatment to reverse her son's autism.

Dr. Campbell-McBride's book is a culminating factor as to why some experts attribute our family's swift results in reversing Brandon's autism naturally. Brandon's progress amazed doctors in a matter of four months after detoxification.

My son and daughter-in-law shared their assessment of Brandon since his detox and training:

> Brandon is independent. He's able to communicate, so we can better fulfill his wants and needs. Now, Brandon has an improved chance of being an independent adult. Brandon also has an increased understanding of what is required of him. He has basically done a complete turn-around. We don't have to constantly monitor him. Before he started his homeopathic medicine, you had to monitor him 24/7. Now, you can leave him with others, and he is interacting with his peers. He's such a joy with a great personality. It's a remarkable difference, and he's a blessing.

"Gut and Psychology Syndrome," has allowed our family to understand every aspect of Brandon's autism from his head to toes, inside his body and out, and also the social, emotional and educational aspects of helping a child with autism.

CHAPTER 9—

KEEPING BRANDON STRONG... "HAPPY CLEANING!!!"

Everything pertaining to keeping Brandon happy and healthy environmentally-wise comes straight from the "Gut and Psychology Syndrome"... Natural Treatment for Autism, Dyspraxia, A.D.D., Dyslexia, A.D.H.D, Depression, Schizophrenia". Dr. Campbell-McBride, MMedSci(neurology), MMedSci(nutrition).

In order to reduce Brandon's general toxic load, we bathe in him in warm water and Epson salt. We use fragrance-free, organic soaps. To prevent dryness, we mix a dab of petroleum jelly and fragrance-free baby lotion. We brush Brandon's teeth with organic toothpaste or a pinch of baking soda.

(Below is an excerpt from the *Detoxification of People with GAP* chapter of "Gut and Psychology Syndrome", pages 207-211.)

The general toxic load

An important part of the treatment is reduction in **the general toxic load** on the patient's detoxification system as much as possible. What is a general toxic load? Anything toxic we eat, breathe, touch, or put on our skin absorbs very quickly and puts another workload on our detoxification system. In a GAPS person his or her gut is the major source of toxicity overloading the detox system with too much work. It is not sensible to add more to that work by exposing the patient to toxic and carcinogenic substances from the environment. What substances are we talking about?

The patient's house should be kept as chemical free as possible by using minimal amounts of domestic cleaning chemicals, paints, carpet pesticides and other toxic substances. All widely available domestic chemicals are toxic. Bathroom detergents, floor cleaners, polishes, etc. all stay in the air and on the surfaces contributing to the general toxic load on the patient's detox system. Toxic domestic chemicals can be replaced with safer bio-degradable alternatives from various conscientious companies. However, generally try to use as little as possible. A lot of cleaning around the house can be done with just water and a bit of vinegar or lemon juice, bicarbonate of soda and olive oil. You can clean your wood floors with strong tea. You can polish your furniture with a mixture of 1 cup of olive

(CONTINUED - Below is an excerpt from the *Detoxification of People with GAP* chapter of "Gut and Psychology Syndrome", pages 207-211.)

oil with 1/2 a cup of white vinegar. You can pour white wine on red wine spills on your carpet to remove the stain.

It is wise **not** to re-decorate the house or install new carpets or furniture while the patient is trying to detoxify. Paints, many building materials, new carpets, new furniture outgas a plethora of extremely toxic chemicals which we absorb through our lungs, skin and mucous membranes. New carpet can outgas considerable amounts of highly carcinogenic formaldehyde for a few years. New furniture is full of fire retardants, which are great contributors of antimony (a toxic heavy metal) in our systems. Fresh household paints outgas dozens of extremely toxic chemicals into the air of the house for at least six months. Just recently I had a phone call from a parent of an autistic child who, apart from severe autism, had epilepsy. After implementing the GAPS nutritional protocol the seizures disappeared completely and the child was doing very well. Then, unfortunately, the parents decided to paint the walls in the house. The day the painter started work the child had a major epileptic fit. Epilepsy in a majority of cases particularly in children, is caused by toxicity. Obviously, this child's detoxification system was not ready to take an onslaught of the extremely toxic chemicals which we can breathe in from paints.

Very important contributors to the general toxic overload in the body are *cosmetics, toiletries, perfumes and other personal care products.* The personal care products industry is generally not regulated. More than a thousand of various carcinogenic and toxic chemicals are widely used in formulation of shampoos, soaps, toothpaste, cosmetics, perfumes, creams, etc. The old opinion that our skin is a barrier and does not let toxins in has proven to be completely wrong. Human skin absorbs most things from the environment very efficiently, in some cases even better than our digestive system. Toxins, which go into the body through the digestive system, have to pass through the liver, where most of them get broken down and rendered benign. That is why the pharmaceutical industry recently started producing more and more drugs which are applied to the skin as patches, because

(CONTINUED - Below is an excerpt from the *Detoxification of People with GAP* chapter of "Gut and Psychology Syndrome", pages 207-211.)

the skin absorbs them better than the digestive system and they get straight in to the bloodstream without passing the test of the liver. The wide use of personal care products is a major contributor to our cancer epidemic. Children, women and men are unknowingly exposing themselves to huge amounts of carcinogenic substances, which they apply to their skin. A good example is breast cancer. Cells removed from a cancerous breast in many cases are full of aluminum – a toxic heavy metal. Where does all this aluminum come from? Probably from not far away – from the deodorants, absorbed through the skin in the woman's armpits. Recent research into heavy metals showed that when a pregnant animal is exposed to them they accumulate in large amounts in the foetus. That is why it is particularly important for a pregnant or breast-feeding mother to be careful what personal products and cosmetics she puts on her skin, face and hair. In this book we cannot go into the details of all toxins present in our toiletries and cosmetics. But let us list some of the common ones.

- Talc or talcum powder can cause ovarian cancer. Do not use it, particularly on babies!
- Sodium Lauryl (Laureth) Sulfate (SLS) — highly toxic detergent and is present in most shampoos, soaps and toothpaste.
- Fluoride — a terrible poison for every system in the body. Widespread in toothpaste and other dental care products. It is added to some water supplies and given to babies as drops. If you are not familiar with its toxicity I would strongly advise you to learn more about it and avoid it like the plague.
- Titanium Dioxide — carcinogenic.
- Triethanolamine (TEA) and Diethanolamine (DEA) form carcinogenic nitrosamines.
- Lanolin, itself a non-toxic natural substance is often contaminated with DDT and other carcinogenic pesticides.

(CONTINUED - Below is an excerpt from the Detoxification of People with GAP chapter of "Gut and Psychology Syndrome", pages 207-211.)

- Dioxanes are inhaled and absorbed through skin — highly carcinogenic.
- Saccharin — carcinogenic.
- Formaldehyde — a toxic and carcinogenic substance.
- Propylene Glycol — carcinogenic
- Lead, aluminum and other heavy metals are present in many personal care products, particularly in deodorants and make-up.

In patients with GAP Syndrome use of personal care products should be reduced to an absolute minimum. The body does not need washing with soaps, shower gels, or bubble baths. They not only contribute to the general toxic overload, but they also wash off important oils, which protect the skin from infections and drying out.

Washing with water and a sponge should be quite enough.

A child does not need any personal care products apart from natural toothpaste. There are number of companies who produce safe personal care products without harmful substances, listed above.

To assist elimination of toxins through the skin, give your child a bath every night before bed. Instead of bath soaps, add a cup of cider vinegar to the bath, it will help to normalise the pH of the skin and encourage appropriate skin flora, as well as assisting the detoxification process. On alternate days add a cup of Epsom Salt to the bath, which will also assist in the detoxification process. Air your house regularly and let you child spend as much time as possible in the fresh air.

Swimming pools are very toxic places. People generally believe that going to the swimming pool is a healthy exercise. This cannot be further from the truth. Apart from a few rare pools in the world, sterilised with the ozone, the rest of them use chlorine-based chemicals for sterilising the water. Chlorine is a poison, which affects every system in the body, particularly the immune system and liver. It absorbs quite well through the skin. But apart from that a thick layer of chlorine gas is floating above the swimming pool water, which children and adults inhale while swimming. Inhaled chlorine absorbs extremely well through the lungs into the bloodstream. GAPS

(CONTINUED - Below is an excerpt from the *Detoxification of People with GAP* chapter of "Gut and Psychology Syndrome", pages 207-211.)

patients are already very toxic. Swimming in a chlorinated pool would add to that toxicity.

GAPS people should swim in the natural waters of lakes, rivers, and sea instead of the toxic chemical soup of swimming pools. Natural waters are full of life, biological energy from plants and different creatures, minerals, enzymes and many other beneficial substances.

Swimming in natural living water has been prized as a therapy for many health problems for centuries. Obviously, you have to make sure that the water you swim in is as far as possible from any source of industrial pollution.

Washing powders and liquids all stay in the fabric of our clothes, bedding and towels and also contribute to the toxic overload. Try to look for safer ecologically friendly alternatives.

House plants are our great friends when it comes to keeping our houses toxin free. They consume the toxic gases and replace them with oxygen and other beneficial substances. Fill your house with geraniums, ivies, spider plants, Aloe Vera, ficuses and many other varieties of houseplants. The more the merrier, particularly in your bedrooms! Keep your houseplants healthy, don't let them become mouldy, as some GAPS people may react to moulds.

Detoxification and reducing exposure to environmental toxins has to be an important part of the treatment of GAP Syndrome. Normalising gut flora, appropriate nourishing diet, clean water, juicing and avoiding exposure to toxins are the natural measures which work very well and without any side effects!

A healthy body is clean inside!

Happy cleaning!

#   #   #

CHAPTER 10—
EDUCATING BRANDON

V-Tech ® Nitro Notebook

*Learning Resources®
LER #6300
Soft Foam Alphabet Dice*

Our Parental Homework with Brandon

Although Brandon did not play with toys or read books the conventional way, we continued to read, sing and teach him in our traditional way.

We read many stories regarding recovering autistic children and were fascinated to learn the common stories that autistic children were somehow trapped in bodies without the ability to communicate. For children with autism, <u>early intervention is the key</u>. Therefore, along with the wonderful governmental programs, such as Early Steps (18 months to age 3), Head Start (ages 3 to 5 years) and Extended School Year ("ESY"), we conducted our very own educational routines at home.

Electronics

When Brandon was non-verbal, we introduced him to interactive educational toys and computers games (Fisher Price®, Leap Frog® - School Time LeapTop, and V-Tech® Nitro Notebook). These interactive computer games reinforced and taught him words and sentences. The programs stimulated Brandon's mind in a healthy way. Soon after, he independently played with his computers, and he still enjoys them tremendously. Brandon has remarkably learned to multi-task. He simultaneously plays with different computers.

Traditional "Hands-On" Learning

At an early stage, we introduced Brandon to traditional flash cards that include numbers, pictures, words, signs, colors, shapes, books and pictures with gestures. Brandon also enjoyed making words with his alphabet dice. Last summer, he spelled over 300 words using the alphabet dice. (Soft Foam Alphabet Dice)

Soft Foam Alphabet Dice
http://www.learningresources.com/p2p/searchResults.do?method=view&search=basic&keyword=6300&sortby=best&asc=true&page=1)

(Below are excerpts from *Part II* of Dr. Chris Greene's **09/03/2008**, "Wake Up To Nutrition" Radio Show on *Autism* (featuring Lynne George and Stuart Tomc)).

LYNNE GEORGE: … [S]ince March….

DR. CHRIS: And I guess, <u>when I saw Brandon last week</u>, <u>he knew the months of the year, and then he was also—we were asking him mathematic equations, and he was able to respond to those.</u>

LYNNE GEORGE: <u>Yes. He knows 1+1, 2+2, 3+3, 4+4, 5+5.</u> And <u>he under[stands]</u>—the thing is, <u>he just doesn't say it. He knows.</u> <u>Like the words that he knows—the two to three hundred words that he knows, he can you tell you the vocabulary.</u> When I was in Florida with my parents, he wrote the word "hiccup." And we go Brandon, what is that? And he goes, you know [MAKES THE HICCUP SOUND].
[CHUCKLE]

LYNNE GEORGE: And he made the sound. So, everything, he's writing—not writing but spelling the words. He can tell you what it means. That's what so phenomenal.

DR. CHRIS: <u>This is not just rote memorization.</u> <u>What we're seeing is actually understanding</u> of—

LYNNE GEORGE: And processing it.

DR. CHRIS: Processing.

LYNNE GEORGE: Uhm hum.

DR. CHRIS: That's to me, Stuart, the critical thinking skills that we're—that we're starting to re-establish with him that I think is so exciting here.

Unique Introduction, Reinforcement and PRAISE!

To begin with, we purchased a table and chairs conducive to Brandon's size, which allowed him an opportunity to see and explore things at a better advantage. We noticed that his learning flourished at that point.

> ***Dr. Chris:***
> *"[W]hen I saw Brandon last week [August 2008], he knew the months of the year, and then he was also—we were asking him mathematic equations, and he was able to respond to those."*
>
> *"This is not just rote memorization. What we're seeing is actually understanding… ."*

Later on, I taught Brandon the "days of the week" through song and continued singing the tune throughout the day. Next, I reinforced his learning by showing him a visual (calendar). Then, I pointed to each word on the visual while I sang the tune. Once he understood, I spoke the words in regular tone (not singing) and pointed to each word on the visual. Afterward, I had him to make eye contact while he repeated the words.

The next step, I asked him a series of questions relating to the words learned; for example, "Brandon, what are the days of the week?" If he responded correctly with a natural response—not of parrot talk but a proper response that reflects understanding—I moved on. Meanwhile, I reviewed the learned material once a week. Finally, I repeated the process with a new learning task that correlated with the previous lesson.

This technique works!

Learning Is Fun Through Educational Television

Currently, Brandon continues to hunger for knowledge and emulates his big brother Anthony in school work and play. Brandon energetically responds and initiates play to the point that Anthony now tells Brandon that he is tired but Brandon wishes to play continuously.

Together, Brandon and Anthony enjoy educational television shows, such as *Super Why!*, *Sesame Street*, *Wow Wow Wubbzy*, The *Wonder Pets*, *The Backyardigans*, *Word Girl*, etc.

Above is the list of words that Brandon spelled on May 31, 2008 (written by MamMaw).

Growing up in a family of educators, I knew the importance of education. Dr. Natasha Campbell-McBride's "Gut and Psychology Syndrome" simply reinforced the direction I would take to reach Brandon.

(Below is an excerpt from "Gut and Psychology Syndrome," by Dr. Natasha Campbell-McBride, pages 235-237.)

6. A FEW WORDS ABOUT EDUCATION

Education of GAPS children is a huge subject. It is beyond the scope of this book to cover it in detail. However, it is important to make one point clear. I have seen many parents in my clinic who have put a lot of effort into the physical side of their child's disorder but did not do much in terms of organising their child's education. These children usually do not do as well as the children who had both issues addressed at the same time.

From the moment children are born, what do they do most of the time?

They learn!

Every moment, they are awake, they learn from the environment, from the people around them how to communicate, how to behave appropriately, how to play with toys appropriately, how to play with their peers and later on, as they go to school, they learn how to acquire academic skills. This is one of the most important abilities we human beings are born with – to be able to learn in order to survive and fit in the world.

A normal child learns from the moment it is born. Have you ever observed babies and toddlers? They are like little sponges, listening to everything, watching everybody around them, absorbing every little bit of information from their environment and learning, learning, learning. Their brain cells develop very vital connections and circuits, which would serve these children for the rest of their lives.

GAPS children miss a lot of this learning. Due to their toxicity their brains are not able to process information properly, so these children are not sponges in those very important first formative years. They have normal ears, eyes, taste buds, and sensors in their skin. But all the information these organs receive is then passed to the brain to be processed. A brain clogged with toxicity cannot process this sensory input appropriately, so GAPS children may not hear, see, taste or feel the same way a normal child would do.

(CONTINUED - Below is an excerpt from "Gut and Psychology Syndrome," by Dr. Natasha Campbell-McBride, pages 235-237.)

Highly functioning autistic individuals, who lecture about their disorder, tell us that they cannot hear certain frequencies, that certain sounds hurt their ears, that they may not hear parts of words said to them or hear them in a distorted way. They say that they cannot see certain parts of the light spectrum, some parts of written words, they get lost or disoriented in fractionated light, for example the shadow of a tree or flickering electric lights, some parts of light spectrum hurt them. They describe touch from certain fabrics and people's hands as unpleasant as the "pins and needles" feeling we can get after sitting comfortably. A lot of these autistic individuals say that many foods taste bland for them and the texture of the food can be offensive. All the sensory input from eyes, ears, skin and mouth turns into a jumble in their heads, disorienting sometimes pleasant, sometimes unpleasant and sometimes frightening. That is shy these children develop all sorts of behaviours which look bizarre to us, but would probably make perfect sense if we took into account what happens to the sensory input in their brains. Their brain cells do not develop normal connections and circuits. Instead they develop abnormal brain cell connections and circuits. Some of these circuits show themselves as self-stimulatory behaviour or self-destructive behaviour.

Depending on the severity of the GAPS condition this abnormality in processing sensory input may range from an absence of speech development in an autistic child, for example, to very slight abnormalities in semantics and pragmatics of the language, commonly seen in ADHD/ADD and dyslexia. Many dyslexia children may not show any obvious problems with processing sensory input until they need to learn reading and writing. However, looking back parents of these children would describe other sensory issues, like unusual fears of certain sounds and objects, strange taste preferences and fussiness with food, unexplained tantrums and unusual play routines. Children with ADHD/ADD, apart from their behavioural problems, almost without exception have deficits in pragmatics of language, which may not be obvious to parents, but can be identified on testing. These are the finer points of the language development concerning

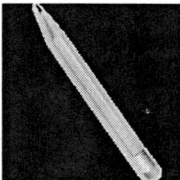

(CONTINUED - Below is an excerpt from "Gut and Psychology Syndrome," by Dr. Natasha Campbell-McBride, pages 235-237.)

conversational skills, answering/responding, greeting, informing, naming, labeling, negotiating, reasoning, etc. This language deficiency leads to problems in social skills and learning.

In the case of severe GAPS like autism the longer this situation goes on for the more normal learning these children miss and the more they fall behind their normal peers. Normal children never stop learning, so for an autistic child to have any chance of catching up with them he or she has to learn at double speed. The earlier this intensive learning starts the more chance there is for an autistic child to catch up simply because he or she misses less. The older the child is the more he or she has missed out and the more he/she has got to catch up on. Apart from learning all the normal things the teaching has to undo all the abnormal patterns and behaviours the child has developed. Again, the older the child the more difficult it becomes to break abnormal brain cell circuits and build normal ones. So there is a definite sense of urgency for parents of newly diagnosed children in starting appropriate education as soon as possible.

The question is – what education?

Let us start from autism, as these children are at the most severe end of the GAP Syndrome.

Helping an Autistic Child

I would not attempt to describe here all the existing methods of educating autistic children. There are many of them and you can find many sources of information on this subject. Some methods aim to create an artificial environment to suit the child's needs. Other methods try to change the child in a way that he or she can fit in the normal world and lead as normal a life as possible. At the end of the day it comes down to parents, their abilities and determination, to what method is chosen.

However, no matter what method is chosen, any educationalist with experience in teaching autistic children would agree, that to be able to achieve the most, an autistic child needs **one-to-one teaching**. This teaching has to be **intensive** and very **structured**. It cannot be just any teaching. It has to be **conducted by specially trained people**. Every skill has to be broken into the tiniest

(CONTINUED - Below is an excerpt from "Gut and Psychology Syndrome," by Dr. Natasha Campbell-McBride, pages 235-237.)

possible steps, manageable for an autistic mind and taught step by step making sure that all the previous steps are solidly learned and used by the child. A normal child would learn every minute he or she is awake, so the teaching has to go on for as **many hours a day as possible**, every day. And we must not forget the sense or urgency if your child stands any chance of catching up with the same age typically developing children. Those children are not standing still in their development, so the goal post is constantly moving. There is not a moment to waste. I personally know only one method, which can achieve all that.

#   #   #

Although, I have difficulties as a result of my back injury, I position myself by either sitting or reclining during Brandon's one-on-one learning commitment. This technique of introducing, reviewing and praising seems to benefit him in different areas of learning. Our learning interaction has become easier since his detox.

Window of Opportunity – Potty-Training

Initially, when I attempted to potty-train Brandon at the age of five years, eight months, he only went to the bathroom when we took him. So, of course, there were plenty of errors which kept him in *Pull-ups*.

Brandon went to the bathroom every 15 to 30 minutes and had three to four bowel movements a day. Ironically, we thought that was a beautiful thing, because, otherwise, Brandon suffered with constipation.

When Brandon's summer school session ended, I thought the 17 days of summer break (July 20 through August 7, 2008) would be the perfect window of opportunity to begin potty training.

Our family was on one accord regarding Brandon's potty schedule. He was not allowed to leave the house during the first week of potty training. We dressed him only in T-shirts, underwear and socks. **Nanna was on potty-patrol!** Every 30 minutes, without touching him in any way, we directed and praised him to and from the bathroom.

Since I was determined to make his "going-to-the-potty" a fun experience, I made a song just for Brandon, which prompted him happily to go to the bathroom.

Potty, potty, potty—potty in the toilet. Brandon is a big boy. He can potty in the toilet!!!!!

I left the bathroom door open, sat nearby and gave him one directive at a time:

(Urination*) Lift the toilet seat. * Flush the toilet. Wash your hands. Dry your hands.

(Defecation* *aka* #2) Put the toilet seat down. * Wipe your bottom. Flush the toilet. Wash your hands. Dry your hands.

As a rule, I entered the bathroom only when it was time for him to wash and dry his hands. We noticed that if Mommy, Daddy, Grandmommie or Nanna (an immediate family member) was in the bathroom while he was doing #2, he wanted that particular person to hold his hand for comfort while he was on his little throne. From an adjacent room, everyone applauded and cheered for a job well done, and Brandon loved the praise.

Each day, the errors were fewer and fewer. <u>By the tenth day/night</u>, no potty errors occurred.

Brandon's next verbal directive was to wash and dry his hands at appropriate times. That one he mastered <u>within two days</u>. After two additional days of reviewing, I added more directives for him to wipe his bottom. Thank goodness, to this day, the nutrients cause him to have healthy bowel movements.

This healthy experience allowed Brandon not to have any smearing on his toilet paper which meant that his gut-brain connection was indeed working. The "no-smearing" part I loved, because it made the correlation of potty-training easy.

Let's Get Dressed!!!

Generally, I taught Brandon to dress himself with the introduction of one item at a time until he mastered it. Again, I praised him for everything. However, at times, if we forgot to praise him, he otherwise would praise himself. We sometimes heard him say, "Good Job, Brandon!" or "Hooray! You did it!" or "Fantastic ... Marvelous!"

Above all, any new thing Brandon does is like a wonderful Christmas present. ***Isn't God good!***

CHAPTER 11—
BRANDON'S SOCIAL SKILLS

nitially, developing Brandon's social skills was difficult. For instance, during outings, if Brandon's older brother or other children were included; we implemented teams—with the possibility of having at least one adult designated to each child. Subsequently, if Brandon grew disruptive during any event, an adult family member was responsible to console him by taking him outside for a walk.

Brandon would not keep still while going to the movies with his family. Seeing a movie in its entirety was mostly out of the question.

At one time, Brandon would not sit in a grocery cart which required his parents to wheel two carts simultaneously—one for groceries and the other for Brandon when he became restless.

Regardless of the difficulties, Brandon went EVERYWHERE with us. His demeanor was not attributed to being mischievous or disobedient. We realized that Brandon's action/reactions were due to his gut-brain connection not being healthy and his frustration of not being able to communicate.

(*See* **APPENDIX B**: Terrebonne Parish Special Education Department)

Due to my disability—not being able to do *many* things independently—I came to the realization of my own limitations. Likewise, Brandon had difficulties of his own. However, I devised ways to reach him.

With this in mind, one of the first things I taught Brandon was the command "Hand". When we said the word "hand", we would pat one hand on the back of the opposite hand. One tap meant for Brandon to "stop". Two taps meant for Brandon to come close or to hold that particular person's hand.

Once the gestures/commands were understood, Brandon knew that he had to obey that particular family member or there would be consequences—"time out".

To reiterate, when Brandon would stim, we would break his stimming cycle with the phrase, "Clap. No flap." This "Clap—No flap" substitution gave him another way of comfortably channeling his emotions.

In addition, saying, "AH-AH" was our friendly "No" to immediately stop Brandon and get his attention.

After Brandon's detoxification process, we noticed that he was more receptive to learn if we made eye contact whenever we spoke to him. This tremendously helped his growth.

Seeing is believing! (*See:* *YouTube* http://www.youtube.com/watch?v=cQPX24s5m8E. Others will be posted in the future.)

CONCLUSION

In summary, Brandon has figured out a thing called "free will." If he does not want to do something, he now tells us "no." He has a personality now—with such sweet spirit and heart. He is an amazing funny-bunny with a kilowatt smile. Everyday he enlightens us with the new things he does or says. He helps us appreciate the little/precious things in life, because, in return, he gives back so much more. We cannot envision life without him.

We thank God for our family, Drs. Chris and Campbell-McBride. We also wish to thank Brandon's therapists and teachers—past and present for their dedication and willingness to their service. We wish to extend a special thanks and consideration to the Louisiana and Georgia departments of education and government. Collectively, you have given our Brandon a new life.

God has shown us that when a door closes, there is always a window of opportunities and gifts if you are willing to believe and work hard.

At the time of this recorded journal, Brandon was five years, nine months.

Brandon's journey is not finished. We hope to continue to with the next chapter of his remarkable life.

THIS IS <u>NOT</u> "THE END!"

REFERENCES

[i]   *Dr. Christopher Greene*
Source: www.wakeuptonutrition.com
Dr. Chris Greene
"WAKE UP TO NUTRITION"
2495 Eastgate Place, Suite A
Snellville, GA 30078
Phone: (770) 979-5825
Toll Free: 1-877-7-AWAKEN
Fax: (770) 979-5834
Email:
Website: www.wakeuptonutrition.com

[ii]   *Stuart Tomc*
Source: www.nordicnaturals.com. Stuart Tomc is an authority on evidence-based dietary supplements with over twenty years experience in the field of Nutritional Medicine. He is a respected consultant to the World Health Organization and integrative physicians worldwide having traveled the world as an educator and trainer for over 10 years. Stuart is adept at educating and delivering a powerful message on important health issues and currently serves as National Educator and Spokesperson for Nordic Naturals. (*See* website: www.nordicnaturals.com.)

[iii]   Nutri-Energetics Systems Scans© ("NES Scans")
Source: http://www.naturalworldhealing.com/nes-description.htm

[iv]   *Laurie Ledbetter*
Source: http://www.guthealth.info
Laurie Ledbetter
US Distributor for Dr. Natasha Campbell-McBride
GUT AND PSYCHOLOGY
P.O. Box 418
Pinelake GA 30072
Phone: (404) 298-9188
Email: laurieledbetter@guthealth.info
Website: http://www.guthealth.info

[v]   *Dr. Daniel Falor*
Source: www.radiohealthnotes.net/drdan.html
"Dr. Daniel Falor earned his BA degree at the University of NY, and then went on to earn his Doctorate of Chiropractic degree from Life Chiropractic College in Marietta, Georgia. After graduating, Dr. Falor was Clinic Director of a successful practice in Loganville, Georgia. In addition to his Chiropractic degree, Dr. Falor has advanced certifications in Nambudripad's Allergy Elimination Technique (NAET), Body Restoration Technique (BRT) and Contact Reflex Analysis (CRA). He has also studied extensively in the field of nutrition and uses many Homeopathic remedies in his quest to provide the best in all-natural health care to his patients. Dr. Falor is pleased to have joined with Dr. Chris Greene at Dr. Chris' Natural Pharmacy, their combined extensive knowledge of nutrition and homeopathy will bring unmatched natural health and wellness care to everyone in the greater Atlanta area."

Dr. Daniel Falor
HOLISTIC HEALTH RESTORATION
11100 Donnington Drive
Duluth, GA 30097
Phone: (770) 401-6065
Email: drfalor@msn.com.

REFERENCES
(CONTINUED)

vi   *Dr. Natasha Campbell-McBride*
Source: www.gutandpsychologysyndrome.com
Dr. Natasha Campbell-McBride MD, MMedSci(neurology), MMedSci(nutrition).
"Natasha Campbell-McBride holds a Degree in Medicine and Postgraduate Degrees in both Neurology and Human Nutrition. In her clinic in Cambridge she specialises in Nutrition for Children and Adults with Behavioural and Learning Disabilities, and Adults with Digestive and Immune System Disorders. Her son was diagnosed with autism."
Contact: info@gutandpsychologysyndrome.com

Campbell-McBride, Dr. Natasha. <u>Gut and Psychology Syndrome</u>. United Kingdom: Medinform Publishing, 2007." (ISBN 0-9548520-0-1)

vii   *Dr. Christopher Greene*
Source: Dr. Chris Greene
Dr. Chris' Natural Pharmacy
1982 E. Main Street/Hwy 78 #D
Snellville, GA 30078
Phone: (770) 979-5125
Fax: (770) 979-6911
New Phone Number for Mail Orders: (770) 979-5825

Listen Live on the Internet: "To Your Health with Dr. Chris Greene"
WGUN Ten click on "Listen Live" button
Radio 1010 AM (Monday thru Friday,11:00 am to 12:00 pm EST)

Call-in Number: (770) 491-7748

APPENDICES

APPENDICES

Appendix A –   Early Steps

Appendix B –   Terrebonne Parish Special Education Department

Appendix C –   2008 Atlanta, Dekalb County, Georgia schools

Appendix D –   Dr. Chris Greene (Appointments)

Appendix E –   09/02/2008 Written Transcript of Dr. Chris Greene's "Wake Up To Nutrition" Radio Show (featuring Lynne George and Laurie Ledbetter)

Appendix F –   09/03/2008 Written Transcript of Dr. Chris Greene's "Wake Up To Nutrition" Radio Show (featuring Lynne George and Stuart Tomc)

APPENDIX A

EARLY STEPS

APPENDIX A
EARLY STEPS

early teps
louisiana's early intervention system

July 2, 2004

Dear

Thank You for your recent referral to earlysteps, Louisiana's Early Intervention System. Part C Early Intervention is dedicated to empowering families who have children with a disability and/or developmental delay. We are excited to start Brandon through our eligibility process. We look forward to guiding you and Brandon to a successful beginning.

Sincerely,

Becky

Becky
Specialist Intake Coordinator

Ages & Stages Questionnaires: A Parent-Completed, Child-Monitoring System

Second Edition

By Diane Bricker and Jane Squires

with assistance from Linda Mounts, LaWanda Potter, Robert Nickel, Elizabeth Twombly, and Jane Farrell

Copyright © 1999 by Paul H. Brookes Publishing Co.

◆ 18 Month ◆ Questionnaire

Please provide the following information.

Child's name: _____ Brandon _____

Child's date of birth: _____ 11 _____ 02 _____

Child's corrected date of birth (if child is premature, add weeks of prematurity to child's date of birth): _____

Today's date: _____ 7-12-04 _____

Person filling out this questionnaire: _____

What is your relationship to the child? _____ mother _____

Your telephone: _____

Your mailing address: _____

City: _____

State: _____ LA _____

ZIP code: _____

List people assisting in questionnaire completion: _____

Administering program or provider: _____ Early Steps -Becky _____

ASQ

Ages & Stages Questionnaires, Second Edition, Bricker et al.
© 1999 Paul H. Brookes Publishing Co.

At this age, many toddlers may be cooperative when asked to do things. You may need to try the following activities with your child more than one time. If possible, try the activities when your child is cooperative. If your child can do the activity but refuses, score "yes" for the item.

		YES	SOMETIMES	NOT YET

COMMUNICATION   *Be sure to try each activity with your child.*

1. When your child wants something, does she tell you by pointing to it?

2. When you ask him to, does your child go into another room to find a familiar toy or object? (You might ask, "Where is your ball?" or say, "Bring me your coat" or "Go get your blanket.")

3. Does your child imitate a two-word sentence? For example, when you say a two-word phrase, such as "Mama eat," "Daddy play," "Go home," or "What's this?" does your child say both words back to you? (Check "yes" even if her words are difficult to understand.)

4. Does your child say eight or more words in addition to "Mama" and "Dada"?

5. Without showing him first, does your child point to the correct picture when you say, "Show me the kitty," or ask, "Where is the dog?" (He needs to identify only one picture correctly.)

6. Does your child say two or three words that represent different ideas together, such as "See dog," "Mommy come home," or "Kitty gone"? (Don't count word combinations that express one idea, such as "Bye-bye," "All right," and "What's that?")

Please give an example of your child's word combinations: _____

COMMUNICATION TOTAL ___ 5

GROSS MOTOR   *Be sure to try each activity with your child.*

1. Does your child bend over or squat to pick up an object from the floor and then stand up again without any support?

2. Does your child move around by walking, rather than by crawling on her hands and knees?

3. Does your child walk well and seldom fall?

4. Does your child climb on an object such as a chair to reach something he wants?

5. Does your child walk down stairs if you hold onto one of her hands? (You can look for this at a store, on a playground, or at home.)

6. When you show him how to kick a large ball, does your child try to kick the ball by moving his leg forward or by walking into it? (If your child already kicks a ball, check "yes" for this item.)

GROSS MOTOR TOTAL ___

5

ASQ

18 months

FINE MOTOR
Be sure to try each activity with your child.

1. Does your child throw a small ball with a forward arm motion? (If he simply drops the ball, check "not yet" for this item.)

2. Does your child stack a small block or toy on top of another one? (You could also use spools of thread, small boxes, or toys that are about 1 inch in size.)

3. Does your child make a mark on the paper with the *tip* of a crayon (or pencil or pen) when trying to draw?

4. Does your child stack three small blocks or toys on top of each other by herself? (You can also use spools of thread, small boxes, or toys that are about 1 inch in size.)

5. Does your child turn the pages of a book by himself? He may turn more than one page at a time.

6. Does your child get a spoon into her mouth right side up so that the food usually doesn't spill?

FINE MOTOR TOTAL

PROBLEM SOLVING
Be sure to try each activity with your child.

1. Does your child drop several (six or more) small toys into a container, such as a bowl or box? (You may show him how to do it.)

2. After you have shown her how, does your child try to get a small toy that is slightly out of reach by using a spoon, stick, or similar tool?

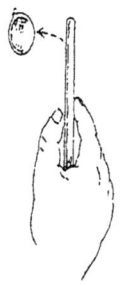

3. After a crumb or Cheerio is dropped into a bottle, does your child purposely turn the bottle over to dump it out? You may show him how to do this. You can use a plastic soda-pop bottle or baby bottle.

4. Without first showing her how, does your child scribble back and forth when you give her a crayon (or pencil or pen)?

5. After he watches you draw a line from the top of the paper to the bottom with a crayon (or pencil or pen), does your child copy you by drawing a single line on the paper in *any direction*? (Scribbling back and forth does not count as "yes.")

Count as "yes"

Count as "not yet"

PROBLEM SOLVING (continued)

6. After a crumb or Cheerio is dropped into a small, clear bottle, does your child turn the bottle upside down to dump out the crumb or Cheerio? (Do not show her how.)

"If problem solving item 6 is marked "yes" or "sometimes," mark problem solving item 3 as "yes."

PROBLEM SOLVING TOTAL   40

PERSONAL-SOCIAL   Be sure to try each activity with your child.

1. While looking at himself in the mirror, does your child offer a toy to his own image?

2. Does your child play with a doll or stuffed animal by hugging it?

3. Does your child get your attention or try to show you something by pulling on your hand or clothes?

4. Does your child come to you when she needs help, such as with winding up a toy?

5. Does your child drink from a cup or glass, putting it down again with little spilling?

6. Does your child copy the activities you do, such as wipe up a spill, sweep, shave, or comb hair?

PERSONAL-SOCIAL TOTAL   35

OVERALL   Parents and providers may use the space at the bottom of the next sheet for additional comments.

1. Do you think your child hears well? ___ not sure   YES ☐   NO ☐

   If no, explain: ___

2. Do you think your child talks like other toddlers his age?   YES ☐   NO ☐

   If no, explain: ___

3. Can you understand most of what your child says?   YES ☐   NO ☐

   If no, explain: ___

4. Do you think your child walks, runs, and climbs like other toddlers her age?   YES ☐   NO ☐

   If no, explain: ___

5. Does either parent have a family history of childhood deafness or hearing impairment?   YES ☐   NO ☐

   If yes, explain: ___

Ages & Stages Questionnaires, Second Edition, Bricker et al.
© 1999 Paul H. Brookes Publishing Co.

ASQ   18 months

OVERALL. (continued)

6. Do you have concerns about your child's vision?   YES ☐   NO ☒

   If yes, explain: _____

7. Has your child had any medical problems in the last several months?   YES ☒   NO ☐

   If yes, explain: _____ custom brain _____

8. Does anything about your child worry you?   YES ☒   NO ☐

   If yes, explain: _____ cut _____

earlySteps
louisiana's early intervention system

Family Assessment of Concerns, Priorities and Resources

EarlySteps is designed to help families increase their abilities to enhance their child's growth and development. To do this, we need to find out what activities your family participates in and which of the activities are most problematic or concerning to you. EarlySteps uses this information to better understand your child's needs and what is most important to your family. This assessment of your concerns, priorities and resources is voluntary—that is, you can decide not to share this information with EarlySteps. We will continue to work with you and your child to determine eligibility.

Assessment of Family Concerns, Priorities, and Resources to enhance development of their child

Date completed: ___7-7-05___

Check appropriate box ☐ Family assessment completed with family concurrence.

☐ Family declined family assessment of concerns, priorities and resources (Parent signature) _____

This assessment is divided into four sections:

1. Family View of Child's Development—You will be asked to tell the Intake Coordinator or Family Support Coordinator what you think about your child's growth and development. While it is important to think about the whole child, you will be asked to talk about specific areas your child's development. EarlySteps often calls these areas developmental domains

2. Family Activities—this section addresses those activities that your family frequently does. You will be asked to think about those activities that are most important to you and if you have any concerns with how your child participates in that activity. You may want to talk about activities that you would like to do but feel you can't because it's too hard or you fear that the activity would not be successful for your child.

3. Daily Living Routines—all children and families have similar routines of daily life. Daily life routines are things like sleeping or napping, eating, dressing, etc. You will be asked to think about the routines of your child's day—the routines may occur at home or in other settings like childcare, grandma's house, etc. We would like you to tell us if any of those routines are concerning to you.

4. Family Resources—EarlySteps is a partnership with families. Your family has resources that can be used to help with the interventions strategies we decide to use with your child. Resources include people (like relatives, sisters and brothers, friends, church members, etc skills you or other family members have, or other things you feel help you.

The Intake Coordinator or Family Service Coordinator will ask you questions in each of the areas listed above. She will take notes on this form. The form has checkboxes to help fill it out quickly—the important part of the form are the boxes where your answer are written, Afterwards, the document will be shared with you so that you can be sure that your statements and thoughts were accurately captured. You will receive a copy of this completed document. Both you and the rest of the EarlySteps team will refer to the information on this document as they work with you during the eligibility determination. If your child found eligible for EarlySteps, this information will be used as you and other members of the team develop the Individualized Family Service Plan. The FS working with you will update this form on a regular basis so that the IFSP team has information about the changing needs of your child and family.

Family's View of Child's Development

This section assists the Early Steps team to learn more about the child's development and your ncerns about your child's growth and development. The information will help with the eligibility determination and, if your child is eligible for EarlySteps, the formation will help establish priorities to address in the Individualized Family Service Plan.

hat concern(s) does the family have about their child's development? (Discuss all developmental domains):

ysical:	1. Tell me about your child's ability to move: Brandon moves easily. He's a "true boy" he runs, jumps, walks, climbs, scoots on the floor.	Do you have a concern about this? no
	2. Tell me about your child's growth: Height & weight is normal. He take a Vitamin everyday	Do you have a concern about this? no
	3. Tell me about your child's ability to see: He sees fine, far away & close. parent has no concerns.	Do you have a concern about this? no
	4. Tell me about your child's ability to hear: Fine. Brandon comes when call him, acknowledges his name.	Do you have a concern about this? no
munication	Tell me how your child lets you know what he/she wants or needs: Brandon will pull you to what he wants, hand gestures.	Do you have a concern about this? yes

Social/Emotional	Tell me about how your child expresses happiness, sadness, frustration, and how he/she calms, etc.: Frustrated - he cries Sad - cries happy - laughs, plays Adjusting to new things is a concern	Do you have a concern about this? ~~No~~ error Hirk yes
Adaptive	Tell me how your child takes care of himself—feeding, sleeping, dressing self, etc.: Brandon finger feeds himself, uses a sippy cup He's starting to understand the potty He helps with dressing	Do you have a concern about this? yes - feeding
Cognitive	Tell me how your child solves problems like getting a toy (he)/she wants: He uses his own imagination, knows where his toys are, know how to turn the TV off + on, likes to play chase.	Do you have a concern about this? NO

April 2005

18 MONTH ASQ Information Summary

Child's name: Brandon

Person filling out the ASQ:

Mailing address:

Telephone:

Today's date: 7-12-04

Date of birth: 11- -02

Corrected date of birth:

Relationship to child: Mother

Assisting in ASQ completion:

City: ___ State: LA ZIP:

OVERALL: Please transfer the answers in the Overall section of the questionnaire by circling "yes" or "no" and reporting any comments.

1. Hears well?
   Comments: not sure
   YES   (NO)

2. Talks like other toddlers?
   Comments:
   YES   NO

3. Understand child?
   Comments:
   YES   NO

4. Walks, runs, and climbs like others?
   Comments:
   (YES)   NO

5. Family history of hearing impairment?
   Comments:
   YES   (NO)

6. Vision okay?
   Comments:
   (YES)   NO

7. Recent medical problems? cyst on brain
   Comments:
   (YES)   NO

8. Other concerns? cyst
   Comments: cyst
   (YES)   NO

SCORING THE QUESTIONNAIRE

1. Be sure each item has been answered. If an item cannot be answered, refer to the ratio scoring procedure in *The ASQ User's Guide.*
2. Score each item on the questionnaire by writing the appropriate number on the line by each item answer.
   YES = 10   SOMETIMES = 5   NOT YET = 0
3. Add up the item scores for each area, and record these totals in the space provided for area totals.
4. Indicate the child's total score for each area by filling in the appropriate circle on the chart below. For example, if the total score for the Communication area was 50, fill in the circle below 50 in the first row.

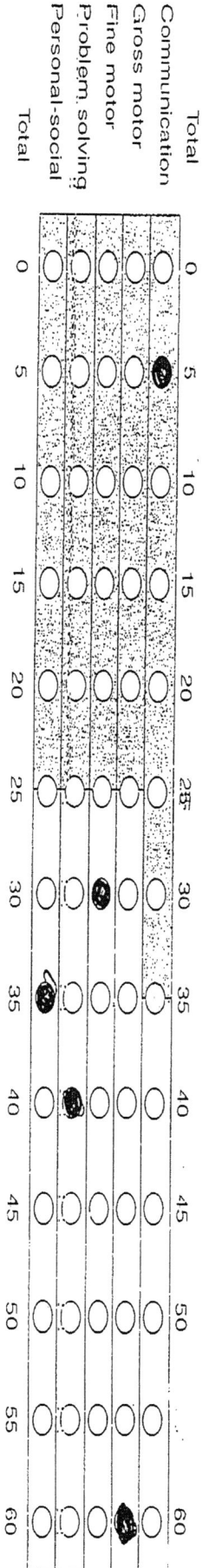

	0	5	10	15	20	25	30	35	40	45	50	55	60
Communication	○	●	○	○	○	○							
Gross motor	○	○	○	○	○	○	●	○	○	○	○	○	○
Fine motor	○	○	○	○	○	○	○	●	○	○	○	○	○
Problem solving	○	○	○	○	○	○	○	○	●	○	○	○	○
Personal-social	○	○	○	○	○	○	○	○	○	○	○	○	●

Total: 0   5   10   15   20   25   30   35   40   45   50   55   60

5. Examine the blackened circles for each area in the chart above.
6. If the child's total score falls within the ▢ area, the child appears to be doing well in this area at this time.
   If the child's total score falls within the ▢ area, talk with a professional. The child may need further evaluation.

OPTIONAL: The specific answers to each item on the questionnaire can be recorded below on the summary chart.

18 months

	Score	Cutoff
Communication	5	35.0
Gross motor	40	25.0
Fine motor	30	25.0
Problem solving	40	25.0
Personal-social	35	25.0

Communication
	1	2	3	4	5	6	Y	S	N

Gross motor
	1	2	3	4	5	6	Y	S	N

Fine motor
	1	2	3	4	5	6	Y	S	N

Problem solving
	1	2	3	4	5	6	Y	S	N

Personal-social
	1	2	3	4	5	6	Y	S	N

Is there anything you think we should know about your child's growth or development that we haven't talked about?

Brandon's eating habits are a concern.

Mom is about to start working on potty-training

Part 2: Family Routines and Activities

EarlySteps is designed to support you and your child with the routines and naturally occurring activities of daily life. The important routines and activities are the targets of any service you and your family receives in EarlySteps. All families have activities that they do on a frequent basis. Think about those activities that your family does and if any of them standout. Do you have any concerns with some of the activities that you do or are there barriers present that keep you from participating in the activity?

Activity	What's happening now? N/A	Area of development impacted by activity (check as needed)
o attending religious events o visiting relatives or friends o going to the library o gardening or fitness activities o attending siblings activities o shopping o family meals o meal prep and clean up o recreation (playing games, watching TV, listening to music, etc) o other:	What is your child doing now during this activity? What can your child do by him or herself during this activity? How does your child get along with others during this activity?	____Physical ____Cognitive ____Communication ____Social or Emotional ____Adaptive
Activity	What's happening now?	Area of development impacted by activity
attending religious events visiting relatives or friends going to the library gardening or fitness activities attending siblings activities shopping family meals meal prep and clean up recreation (playing games, watching TV, listening to music, etc) other:	What is your child doing now during this activity? What can your child do by him or herself during this activity? How does your child get along with others during this activity?	____Physical ____Cognitive ____Communication ____Social or Emotional ____Adaptive
tivity	What's happening now?	Area of development

Part 3: Daily Living Routines   Think about those routines that your child does everyday and if any of them standout. Do you have any concerns with som of the routines that you do or are there barriers present that keep your child from being successful?

Type of Routine	What's your child doing during the routine? Brandon is just starting to become familiar w/ the potty.	Area of Development impacted by the activity
Daily living Activities ☐ bathing ☐ dressing ☐ eating ☒ potty training ☐ playing indoors ☐ playing outdoors ☐ sleeping/napping	What is your child doing now during this activity? he pulls the seat up + down he screams if you put him on the potty, but will sit on it with the What can your child do by him or herself during this activity? lid down. How does your child get along with others during this activity? Presently he cries and screams. He only sits on the toilet with the	_____ Physical _____ Cognitive _____ Communication _____ Social or Emotional _____ Adaptive
Type of Routine	What's your child doing during the routine? toilet seat down.	Area of Development impacted by the activity
Daily living Activities ☐ bathing ☐ dressing ☐ eating ☐ potty training ☐ playing indoors ☐ playing outdoors ☐ sleeping/napping	What is your child doing now during this activity? N/A What can your child do by him or herself during this activity? How does your child get along with others during this activity?	_____ Physical _____ Cognitive _____ Communication _____ Social or Emotional _____ Adaptive

Part 4: Family Resources All families have resources (people, skills, things) that help to support them. Sometimes others easily see the resources and sometimes the resource may be hidden within a person. Tell us about the resources you have to help you with your child.

Mom is in school, dad is employed, housing, transportation, family support

Our family's priorities to address are:

Speech & language development
feeding skills/eating habits
adjusting to new things.

This is the end of the Family Assessment of Concerns, Resources and Priorities. Thank you for your information and time

Information provided by: MOM

Signature

Date: 7-7-05

APPENDIX B

TERREBONNE PARISH SPECIAL EDUCATION DEPARTMENT

State of Louisiana Universal Certificate of Immunizations

Expiration Date: 11 /2013   Vaccine: DTaP/DT/Td/Tdap*
This record is invalid without a proper expiration date

Childs Name: BRANDON P
SIIS Patient ID: 1981095

Date of Birth:

Parent or Guardian:

Vaccine	MONTH, DAY AND YEAR EACH DOSE WAS GIVEN						
	Dose 1	Dose 2	Dose 3	Dose 4	Dose 5	Dose 6	Dose 7
DTaP/DTP/Td	06/26/2003	09/30/2003	06/08/2004	12/05/2006			
OPV/IPV	06/26/2003	12/18/2003	12/05/2006				
MMR	12/18/2003	12/05/2006					
Hib	06/26/2003	09/30/2003	12/18/2003				
Hep B - 3 Dose	11/25/2002	12/18/2003	12/05/2006				
Varicella	06/08/2004	12/05/2006					
Pneumo (PCV7)	06/26/2003	09/30/2003					

* **School Entry Complete-Minimum:** 4-DTP, 3-Polio,(last DTP and Polio after 4th birthday), 2-MMR after 1st birthday and, 3-Hep B
** **Daycare Center:** Hib also required
*** Beginning Aug 2003, Varicella vaccine or history of the disease will be required for school and daycare entry.
**** As a result of Hurricanes Katrina and Rita in 2005, many immunization records were destroyed or lost. Impacted children should be considered up-to-date for enrollment as long as they show proof of having received age-appropriate immunizations.
Varicella History:

I certify that this child has received the above noted immunizations and is in compliance with rules set forth by the State of Louisiana. Department of Health and Hospitals, Office of Public Health until the expiration date above.

Sonya

Authorized Signature

September 30, 2008

Date

TERREBONNE PEDIATRIC AND TEEN CLINIC

Clinic of Issue

Falsification of this record could result in imprisonment for not more than five years or by a fine of not more than five thousand dollars, or both, pursuant to R.S. 14:132 or R.S. 14:133.

GARS

Gilliam Autism Rating Scale

SUMMARY/RESPONSE FORM

Section I. Identifying Information

Subject's Name _Brandon_

Address _____

Parents'/Guardians' Names _____

School _____

Examiner's Name _____

Examiner's Title _____

	Year	Month
Date of GARS Rating		
Subject's Date of Birth		
Subject's Age		

Section II. Score Summary

Subtests	Raw Score	SS	%ile	SE$_M$
Stereotyped Behaviors	13	8	25	1
Communication	18	10	50	1
Social Interaction	4	3	1	1
Developmental	3	7	16	1
Sum of Standard Scores	28		9	
Autism Quotient	80		9	3

Section III. Interpretation Guide

Subtest Standard Scores	Autism Quotient	Degree of Severity	Probability of Autism
		High	
17–19	131+		Very High
15–16	121–130		High
13–14	111–120		Above Average
8–12	90–110		Average
6–7	80–89		Below Average
4–5	70–79		Low
1–3	≤69		Very Low
		Low	

Section IV. Profile of Scores

© 1995 by PRO-ED, Inc.

11 12 13 14 15   04 03

Additional copies of this form (#6822) are available from PRO-ED, 8700 Shoal Creek Blvd., Austin, TX 78757, 512/451-3246.

REEL-3

Receptive–Expressive Emergent Language Test–Third Edition

Section I. Identifying Information

Child's Name _Brandon_

Female ☐   Male ☒

Informants' Names (Parents or caregivers responding to test items) _Anjanette_

Preschool, Daycare, or School _N/A_

School District _Oakshire_

Language(s) Spoken in the Home or Daycare _English_

Examiner's Name _Mandy_

Examiner's Title _Speech-Language Pathologist_

	Year	Month	Day
Date of Testing	2005	08	03
Date of Birth	2002	11	03
Chronological Age	2	8	9
Prematurity Adjustment	–	–	
Corrected Age			
Age in Months		32 mos	

Section II. Record of Scores

	Raw Score	Age Equivalent	Ability Score	%ile Rank	SEM	Confidence Interval	Score Range	Descriptive Rating
Receptive Language	31	9	56	<1	3	68%	53 to 59	very poor
Expressive Language	40	13	+ 63	<1	3	68%	60 to 66	very poor
Sum of Receptive and Expressive Ability Scores			= 119					
Language Ability Score			(51)	<1	3	68%	48 to 54	very poor

Section III. Guidelines for Interpreting the REEL-3 Ability Scores

REEL–3 Ability Score	Description	Percentage Included in Bell-Shaped Distribution
>130	Very Superior	2.34
121–130	Superior	6.87
111–120	Above Average	16.12
90–110	Average	49.51
80–89	Below Average	16.12
70–79	Poor	6.87
<70	Very Poor	2.34

003, 1978 by PRO-ED, Inc.

4 5   07 06 05 04

Additional copies of this form (#10677) may be purchased from
PRO-ED, 8700 Shoal Creek Blvd., Austin, TX 78757-6897
800/897-3202, Fax 800/397-7633, www.proedinc.com

Battelle Developmental Inventory
2nd edition

Name _Brandon_
Last / First / MI

Sex M☒ F☐ ID# _____

Examiner _M_

School/Program _____

Teacher _____ Classroom/Grade _____

Items Administered in: ☒ English Only ☐ Spanish Only ☐ Mixed English and Spanish

Assessment Period: ☐ Beginning of year ☐ Mid-year ☐ End of year

Summary Profile

Domains and Subdomains	Age Equivalent (see Appendix A)	Subdomain Raw Score Totals (from pgs 4–28)	Subdomain Percentile Rank (See Appendix B)	Subdomain Scaled Score (See Appendix B)	Sum of Subdomain Scaled Scores
Adaptive (ADP)					
Self-Care (SC)					
Personal Responsibility (PR)				+	
Total				=	
Personal-Social (P-S)					
Adult Interaction (AI)					
Peer Interaction (PI)				+	
Self-Concept and Social Role (SR)				+	
Total				=	
Communication (COM)					
Receptive Communication (RC)	0-7	15	<1	1	
Expressive Communication (EC)	0-8	13	<1	+ 1	
Total				= 2	
Motor (MOT)					
Gross Motor (GM)					
Fine Motor (FM)				+	
Perceptual Motor (PM)				+	
Total				=	
Cognitive (COG)					
Attention and Memory (AM)					
Reasoning and Academic Skills (RA)				+	
Perception and Concepts (PC)				+	
Total				=	
BDI-2 Total				=	

	Year	Month	Day
Date of Testing			
Date of Birth			
Chronological Age		*	**
Age in Months***			

***Number of years(*) × 12 + number of months(**). Ignore all days.

2 yrs 8 mos / 32 mos

Conversion Table for Sum of Scaled Score (Appendix C)

95%

	Sum of Scaled Scores	Developmental Quotient	Percentile Rank	Confidence Interval
Adaptive				to
Personal-Social				to
Communication	2	55	0.1	51 to 63
Motor				to
Cognitive				to
BDI-2 Total				to

Developmental Quotient Composite Profile

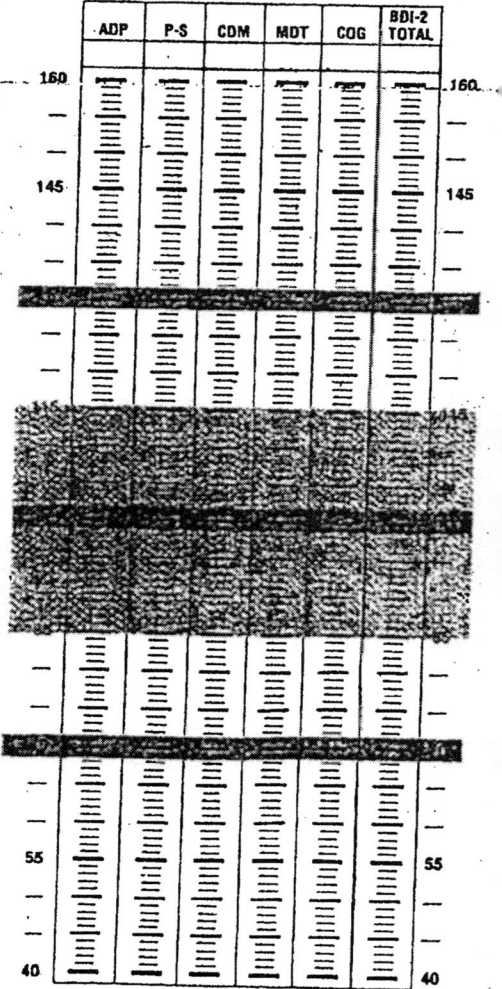

ADP	P-S	COM	MOT	COG	BDI-2 TOTAL

Subdomain Profile – Scaled Scores

SC	PR	AI	PI	SR	RC	EC	GM	FM	PM	AM	RA	PC
Adaptive		Personal-Social			Communication		Motor			Cognitive		

© 2005 LINC Associates, Inc. and The Riverside Publishing Company.

Battelle Developmental Inventory
2nd edition

Name _____ Last

(1) Brandon First   MI

Sex M ☒ F ☐ ID# _____

Examiner _____

School/Program **Oakshire**

Teacher _____   Classroom/Grade _____

Items Administered in: ☐ English Only ☐ Spanish Only ☐ Mixed English and Spanish

Assessment Period: ☐ Beginning of year ☐ Mid-year ☐ End of year

Summary Profile

Domains and Subdomains	Age Equivalent (see Appendix A)	Subdomain Raw Score Totals (from pgs 4–28)	Subdomain Percentile Rank (See Appendix B)	Subdomain Scaled Score (See Appendix B)	Sums of Subdomain Scaled Scores
Adaptive (ADP)					
Self-Care (SC)	13	24	<1	1	
Personal Responsibility (PR)	24	6	16	+ 7	
Total					= 8
Personal-Social (P-S)					
Adult Interaction (AI)	20	36	5	5	
Peer Interaction (PI)		4	1	+ 3	
Self-Concept and Social Role (SR)	21	25	2	+ 4	
Total					= 12
Communication (COM)					
Receptive Communication (RC)					
Expressive Communication (EC)				+	
Total					=
Motor (MOT)					
Gross Motor (GM)	24	58	25	8	
Fine Motor (FM)	14	26	2	+ 4	
Perceptual Motor (PM)		6	<1	+ 1	
Total					= 13
Cognitive (COG)					
Attention and Memory (AM)	16	28	2	4	
Reasoning and Academic Skills (RA)		10	9	+ 6	
Perception and Concepts (PC)	13	12	<1	+ 2	
Total					= 12
BDI-2 Total					=

	Year	Month	Day
Date of Testing	2005	08	03
Date of Birth	2002	11	
Chronological Age	2*	8**	9***
Age in Months***		32	

*** Number of years(*) × 12 + number of months(**). Ignore all days.

Conversion Table for Sum of Scaled Scores (Appendix C)

	Sum of Scaled Scores	Developmental Quotient	Percentile Rank	% Confidence Interval
Adaptive	8	73	4	67 to 83
Personal-Social	12	77	6	73 to 83
Communication	2	55	0.1	51 to 63
Motor	13	70	2	65 to 79
Cognitive	12	68	2	63 to 77
BDI-2 Total				to

Developmental Quotient Composite Profile

	ADP	P-S	COM	MOT.	COG.	BDI-2 TOTAL
160						160
145						145
115						115
85						85
55						55
40						40

Subdomain Profile – Scaled Scores

SC	PR	AI	PI	SR	RC	EC	GM	FM	PM	AM	RA	PC	
Self-Care	Personal Responsibility	Adult Interaction	Peer Interaction	Self-Concept and Social Role	Receptive Communication	Expressive Communication	Gross Motor	Fine Motor	Perceptual Motor	Attention and Memory	Reasoning and Academic Skills	Perception and Concepts	
Adaptive		Personal-Social			Communication		Motor			Cognitive			
•	•	•	•	•	•	•	•	•	•	•	•	•	19
•	•	•	•	•	•	•	•	•	•	•	•	•	18
•	•	•	•	•	•	•	•	•	•	•	•	•	17
•	•	•	•	•	•	•	•	•	•	•	•	•	15
•	•	•	•	•	•	•	•	•	•	•	•	•	14
•	•	•	•	•	•	•	•	•	•	•	•	•	13
•	•	•	•	•	•	•	•	•	•	•	•	•	12
•	•	•	•	•	•	•	•	•	•	•	•	•	11
•	•	•	•	•	•	•	•	•	•	•	•	•	9
•	•	•	•	•	•	•	•	•	•	•	•	•	8
•	•	•	•	•	•	•	•	•	•	•	•	•	7
•	•	•	•	•	•	•	•	•	•	•	•	•	6
•	•	•	•	•	•	•	•	•	•	•	•	•	5
•	•	•	•	•	•	•	•	•	•	•	•	•	3
•	•	•	•	•	•	•	•	•	•	•	•	•	2
•	•	•	•	•	•	•	•	•	•	•	•	•	1

Battelle Developmental Inventory

SCREENING TEST SCORING BOOKLET

9-21377

Name _Brandon_

School/Program _____

Teacher _____

Examiner _Trudy_

	Yr.	Mo.	Day
Date of Testing	2005	5	31
Date of Birth	2002	11	
Chronological age	2	6	13
Age In Months _30_			(12 x years + months; ignore all days)

SCORE SUMMARY

Domain	Raw Score	Standard Deviation (−1, −1.5, −2.0)	Cutoff Score (Table N-53)	Decision Pass	Decision Fail*	Age Equivalent (Tables N-54 and N-55)
Personal-Social	8		20		✓	
Adaptive	13		16		✓	
Gross Motor	8		7	✓		
Fine Motor	8		8 -		✓	
Motor						
Receptive	4		7		✓	
Expressive	4		7		✓	
Communication	8		14		✓	
Cognitive	12		15		✓	
Total Score						

*Recommendations:

- Some autistic tendencies
- Would not separate from mom
- Cried most of the testing time
- he will go get what he wants or he will pull mom's hand to get what he wants to express his wants or needs at home according to mom
- he babbles alot during the screening at home
- mom says he will repeat the t.v. shows at home
- had difficulty transitioning from one task to another task
- he did use eye contact + looked up when his name was called.

9 10 11 12 13 14–DFP–06 05 04 03

Copyright © 1984, 1988 LINC Associates, Inc.
Reproduction of this form without prior written permission is a violation of copyright law.

Riverside Publishing
A HOUGHTON MIFFLIN COMPANY

TERREBONNE PARISH SCHOOL BOARD
Special Education Department
FULL AND EFFECTIVE NOTICE
Individual Evaluation

BRANDON
_____
STUDENT

October 24, 2005
_____
DATE

Oakshire Elementary
_____
SCHOOL AREA

Enclosed is a copy of your child's Individual Evaluation Report. This report summarizes all data collected during the screening and assessment phase of your child's evaluation. You should examine the report carefully and note any questions you may have regarding the results. If you would like an opportunity for an oral explanation, please call:

Patricia
EVALUATION COORDINATOR
(985) 851-

The classification in the report is determined by the criteria established by the Louisiana State Department of Education in the Pupil Appraisal Handbook. If your child meets the criteria to receive special education services or if a change in his/her special education program is needed, a meeting will be scheduled to develop an Individual Education Program (IEP). The Special Education Department will contact you within thirty (30) days of this letter to schedule an appointment to discuss the education plans for your child.

Sincerely,

Patricia

Evaluation Coordinator

APPROVED:

Melissa
_____
Special Education Supervisor
Melissa

Marie
_____
Pupil Appraisal Coordinator
Marie

LOUISIANA PUBLIC SCHOOLS
PUPIL APPRAISAL SERVICES
INDIVIDUAL EVALUATION / INTEGRATED REPORT

OCTOBER 24, 2005
DATE OF REPORT / DISSEMINATION

STUDENT'S NAME:	**BRANDON**
SS#:	
AGE:	**2 YEARS, 11 MONTHS**
DATE OF BIRTH:	11 '02
RACE:	Black
SEX:	Male
PARENT'S NAME:	
PARENT'S ADDRESS:	
PHONE:	
SCHOOL DISTRICT:	TERREBONNE PARISH
SCHOOL AREA:	*Oakshire Elementary Area*
GRADE:	PS
CURRENT TEACHER:	N/A
EVALUATION COORDINATOR:	**Patricia**

REASONS FOR REFERRAL

Brandon has been receiving early intervention services under Part C of the Infant and Toddler Act through Louisiana Early Steps. Brandon is approaching his third birthday and it is necessary to evaluate Brandon to determine whether he qualifies for further services under the Child Search System.

SCREENINGS

Vision and hearing screenings were conducted within the past year and found to be within normal limits.

A health screening was conducted and yielded at-risk results. Brandon was referred for a health assessment. Results of that assessment are contained within this report.

An assistive technology screening on 08/03/05 indicated Brandon was at-risk in communication functioning and that low technology methods could meet his needs at this time. Assistive technology needs and recommendations are incorporated within the speech/language section of this report.

A developmental screening was conducted utilizing the <u>Battelle Developmental Inventory Edition, Screening Test</u>. Brandon's development appeared normal in the area of gross motor.

Further assessment was warranted in the areas of adaptive, personal-social, communication, fine motor, and cognitive.

A review of Brandon's educational history revealed that, although Brandon has received early intervention services through Early Steps, he has never been enrolled in a public school setting. Because Brandon is not enrolled in school, no classroom interventions have been conducted. No previous standardized test scores were available for review.

HEALTH ASSESSMENT

Brandon was referred for a health assessment. He has a diagnosis of a left temporal lobe cyst. In the school setting Brandon will require diapering and assistance with oral feeding. According to parent interview, his health is good with no illnesses or hospitalizations. In March 2004, the cyst in his left temporal lobe was found. At this time, there is no need for surgery. Brandon goes to his physician for regular checkups to check the growth of the cyst.

He appeared to be a well-nourished, well-developed male who was clean and dressed appropriately for age and weather. Past health history revealed one ear infection without PE tubes. According to his mother, he is not restricted in his diet, but is a picky eater. He is able to feed himself finger foods, but will require assistance with a fork and spoon. He is in the process of being potty trained, but will need diapering or toileting in the school setting. His primary physician is Dr. . / and Terrebonne General Medical Center is the preferred hospital in the event of an emergency at school. Brandon cannot participate in contact sports or "roughhousing" play. If he receives a blow to his head, his parents should be notified immediately. An ISHP and emergency plan will be written and presented at the time of the IEP meeting.

FAMILY INTERVIEW

Brandon's mother was interviewed to determine the impact of social, cultural, developmental, and/or health factors that seem to contribute to Brandon's difficulties. She expressed concern with communication difficulties and Brandon's lack of interpersonal skills in making friends and interacting with others. Community services already obtained include Medicaid, SSI, Family Service Coordination, special instruction from an infant homebased teacher, and speech/language pathology services through Early Steps. Brandon is scheduled to begin receiving occupational therapy in the late month of August through Early Steps.

Brandon was described as a highly independent child. He says very few words. Whenever he wants something, he will get it for himself or will take your hand and pull you to the location of the item. He is able to communicate his wants and needs through gestures, body language, and limited vocalizations.

Ms. _____ reports that Brandon is a sweet child who accepts affection from familiar persons. He prefers a routine schedule, but is generally able to accept changes made in his schedule. Brandon tends to play alone or alongside others. He displays an awareness of other children, but seldom interacts with them. He interacts with his four year old brother and other family members, but does not initiate the interaction.

Brandon was born full-term following a normal pregnancy. Ms. _____ related that the doctor was not present at delivery and Brandon had a lot of mucous at birth.

Brandon's current health is generally good. He has experienced only one ear infection since birth. Health history is significant for a small cyst on his front left temporal lobe. The cyst is being monitored at this time and is not interfering with health or development. No medical treatment is recommended at this time. Brandon does not regularly take any medications.

Parental report indicates that Brandon's developmental milestones were within normal limits except in the area of speech. He crawled at 5 months and walked at 13 months. Brandon's verbal communication is primarily babbling, but he can say some words. He recites some numbers, his ABC's, and sings a few nursery rhymes such as Ring Around the Roses and Itsy Bitsy Spider. Brandon is not toilet-trained.

FUNCTIONAL / DEVELOPMENTAL ASSESSMENT

Brandon was evaluated at the Special Education office with his mother serving as informant. Brandon was 32 months old at the time of assessment. The Battelle Developmental Inventory, 2nd Edition (BDI-2) was utilized to determine Brandon's levels of performance and participation in appropriate activities. The BDI-2 is a standardized, individually administered assessment battery of key developmental skills in children from birth through 7 years of age. The BDI-2 is effective in measuring functional abilities in young children. It is useful in identifying the developmental strengths and opportunities for learning during the critical period of early childhood. Functioning is assessed in four areas or domains. These domains are adaptive, personal-social, motor, and cognitive.

An analysis of participation in appropriate activities include:
- (1) Difficult to engage in assessment activities
- (2) Exhibited limited verbal interaction
- (3) Inadequate attention to tasks
- (4) Results are believed to be reliable estimates of developmental levels

Results of BDI-2 Assessment

	AGE EQUIVALENT	PERCENTILE RANK	DEVELOPMENTAL QUOTIENT
ADAPTIVE		4	73
Self-Care	13 Months	<1	
Personal-Responsibility	24 Months	16	
PERSONAL-SOCIAL		6	77
Adult Interaction	20 Months	5	
Peer Interaction		1	
Self-Concept and Social Role	21 Months	2	

	AGE EQUIVALENT	PERCENTILE RANK	DEVELOPMENTAL QUOTIENT
MOTOR		2	70
Gross Motor	24 Months	25	
Fine Motor	14 Months	2	
Perceptual Motor		<1	
COGNITIVE		2	68
Attention and Memory	16 Months	2	
Reasoning and Academic Skills		9	
Perception and Concepts	13 Months	<1	

The Adaptive Domain measures the child's ability to use the information and skills acquired in the other domains. Self-care milestones consist of activities that move the child from complete dependence on the parent to a self-sufficient, functioning child. Personal Responsibility milestones examine the child's ability to assume responsibility for his or her actions and to move around in his or her environment safely and productively. In the area of adaptive development, Brandon was observed or reported to:

(1)   Feed self bite-sized pieces of food
(2)   Help dress self by holding out arms or legs
(3)   Ask for food or liquid with words or gestures
(4)   Move independently around the house, requiring only occasional supervision
(5)   Understand that hot is dangerous
(6)   Put away toys when asked

Some age appropriate behaviors not observed or reported were:

(1)   Use a spoon or other utensil to feed self
(2)   Remove shoes without assistance
(3)   Drink from a cup without assistance and with little spilling
(4)   Feed self with a spoon or fork without assistance
(5)   Distinguish between food substances and nonfood substances
(6)   Remove clothing unassisted
(7)   Accurately respond "Yes" or "No" when asked if he has to use the toilet
(8)   Express a need to use the toilet
(9)   Control bowel movement regularly

The Personal-Social Domain assesses abilities and characteristics that allow a child to engage in meaningful social interaction with adults and peers and to develop his or her own self-concept and sense of social role. In the area of personal-social development, Brandon was observed or reported to:

(1)   Respond positively to adults praise, rewards, or promise of rewards
(2)   Greet familiar adults spontaneously
(3)   Enjoy having someone read simple stories
(4)   Help with simple household tasks
(5)   Respond positively when familiar adults or adults in authority initiate social contact
(6)   Follow directions related to daily routine
(7)   Appropriately communicate a range of positive and negative emotions
(8)   Show pride in accomplishments
(9)   Express enthusiasm for work or play
(10)   Shows awareness of the presence of other children
(11)   Displays independent behavior

Some age appropriate behaviors that were not observed or reported were:

(1)   Allow others to participate in activities
(2)   Initiate social contact or interactions with familiar adults
(3)   Enjoy playing with other children
(4)   Imitate the play activities of other children
(5)   Respond differently to familiar and unfamiliar children
(6)   Identify self in mirror
(7)   Express ownership or possession
(8)   State first name
(9)   Use objects in make-believe play
(10)   Use words for social contact

The Motor Domain assesses a child's ability to control and use the large and small muscles of the body. In the area of gross motor, Brandon was observed to:

(1) Maintain or correct balance when moving from a standing position to other, nonvertical positions
(2) Walk up and down stairs without assistance
(3) Walk backward 5 feet

The following age appropriate developmental skills were not observed:

(1) Run 10 feet without falling
(2) Kick a ball forward without falling
(3) Throw a ball 5 feet forward with direction

In the area of fine motor, Brandon was able to:

(1) Extend a toy to a person and release it from his grasp
(2) Intentionally propel or throw an object

In the area of fine motor, Brandon was unable to:

(1) Extend or point with index finger independent of the thumb and other fingers
(2) Scribble linear and/or circular patterns spontaneously
(3) Use pads of fingertips to grasp pencil

In the area of perceptual motor, Brandon was able to:

(1) Reach for and touch an object placed in front
(2) Reach for an object with one hand
(3) Intentionally drop a cube into a cup with demonstration

In the area of perceptual motor, Brandon refused or had difficulty when asked to:

(1) Place a raisin in a bottle
(2) Dump a raisin from a bottle
(3) Place 4 rings on a post in any order

The Cognitive Domain measures those skills and abilities most commonly thought of as "mental" or "intellectual," with the exception of language and communication skills. They involve activities such as attending to, perceiving, and processing information; remembering; thinking; and knowing. Achievement of these milestones is related to early success in school-related activities such as reading and mathematics. In the area of cognitive development, Brandon was able to:

(1)   Occupy self for 10 or more minutes without demanding attention
(2)   Look at, point to, or touch pictures in a book
(3)   Attend to one activity for 3 or more minutes
(4)   Show interest and enjoyment in age-appropriate books or printed materials
(5)   Pull a cloth to obtain a object
(6)   Physically explores or investigates his surroundings
(7)   Places a circle and a square in a form board

The following age appropriate developmental skills were not observed:

(1)   Search for a removed object
(2)   Find an object hidden under one of two cups
(3)   Select the hand hiding a toy
(4)   Nest objects inside one another
(5)   Match colors
(6)   Respond to *one* and *one more*
(7)   Imitate simple facial gestures

An analysis of results from the domains administered from the BDI-2 and reported here indicates Brandon's performance falls below the expected level for a child in his age group in the areas of adaptive, personal-social, motor, and cognitive. These delays suggest a need for early educational intervention.

Observation of Brandon's motor development in an unstructured environment revealed he did not respond to directions addressed to him; however, most of the skills were observed. The main concern at this time is socialization and participation skills.

This corroborates the findings that participation in regular physical education is indicated. Brandon's gross motor skills can be addressed within his educational environment. If there are any gross motor concerns in the future, a referral to an adapted physical education teacher may be warranted.

SPEECH / LANGUAGE ASSESSMENT

Brandon's levels of speech and language functioning were assessed through the administration of standardized testing, observation of communication behavior, analysis of a communication sample, oral peripheral examination, and collateral data.

Articulation

Articulation was not fully assessed due to Brandon's limited expressive language abilities. An informal evaluation performed as Brandon sang his favorite songs indicated that articulation errors were present, but they appeared to be developmental in nature at this time. Articulation development should be monitored as Brandon's expressive language abilities improve.

Oral Peripheral Examination

An oral peripheral examination indicated adequate structure for speech production. Oral function was not formally assessed, as Brandon did not readily follow commands given. However, an observation of Brandon's oral function when he vocalized and sang indicated seemingly normal lingual functioning. An open mouth posture at rest was noted inconsistently as well as some drooling. Brandon's oral functioning should be adequate for speech production.

Voice and Fluency

Observation indicated that Brandon's voice appears appropriate for his age and sex in quality, resonance, pitch, and loudness.

No evidence of abnormal irregularities in fluency was noted during his vocalizations and unintelligible jargon, but a complete assessment could not be performed due to Brandon's expressive language difficulties.

Language

Brandon's language skills were assessed through the administration of the Communication Domain of the BDI-2, analysis of a language sample, and observation of Brandon's communication behavior.

The Communication Domain is composed of the Receptive and Expressive Subdomains. Subdomain standard scores are expressed as scaled scores with a mean score of 10 and a standard deviation of 3. The overall Communication standard score is presented as a developmental quotient score with a mean of 100 and a standard deviation of 15. On the communication domain of the BDI-2, Brandon achieved the following age equivalency scores, percentiles, and standard scores:

	AGE EQUIVALENT	PERCENTILE RANK	SCALED SCORE	DEVELOPMENTAL QUOTIENT
TOTAL COMMUNICATION		0.1	2	55
Receptive	7 Months	<1	1	
Expressive	8 Months	<1	1	

Brandon's communication score of 55 falls into the significantly below average range of scores and is indicative of a significant developmental delay in the area of language development.

In the receptive subdomain, Brandon was able to respond to a nonspeech sound outside his field of vision; be soothed by a familiar adult's voice; turn his head toward the source of a sound outside his field of vision; respond with awareness, acceptance, and in socially acceptable ways when a familiar person approaches or talks to him; respond to different tones of a person's voice; associate spoken words with familiar objects or actions; and identify family members when named.

Brandon was not observed to respond to a voice outside his field of vision; attend to someone speaking to him for at least ten seconds; attend to other people's conversation for 30 seconds; respond to simultaneous verbal and gestural commands; look at or point to an object across the room when it is named; and follow 3 or more familiar verbal commands.

In the expressive subdomain, Brandon was able to vocalize to express his feelings; produce one or more single-syllable consonant-vowel sounds in close succession; use gestures to indicate his wants or needs; spontaneously initiate sounds or gestures that are associated with objects in the immediate environment; and use 10 or more words.

Brandon was not observed to wave bye-bye; imitate speech sounds; use variations in his voice; communicate in a back-and-forth, turn-taking style using sounds, gestures, or other nonverbal methods; use 2-word utterances to express meaningful relationships; and use words to express what he sees and does and to express the experiences that immediately affect him.

The Receptive-Expressive Emergent Language Test-Third Edition (REEL-3) was administered to assist with describing Brandon's language difficulties. The REEL-3 is a norm-referenced test appropriate for use with infants and toddlers from birth to 36 months. The test is in the form of a checklist that uses an informant (usually the parent, guardian, or caregiver) to assist in providing information about the child's language behavior. Brandon's mother served as the informant for completion of this test. The REEL-3 has a mean Ability Score (standard score) of 100 with a standard deviation of 15. Results of the REEL-3 follow:

	ABILITY SCORE	PERCENTILE RANK	RATING
Receptive Language	56	< 1	Very Poor
Expressive Language	63	< 1	Very Poor
Language Ability Score	51	< 1	Very Poor

Results of the REEL-3 supported the results of the BDI-2 and indicated significant receptive and expressive language deficits.

In the area of Receptive Language, Brandon was reported to:
(1)   Show signs that he knows what words such as *Daddy, Mama,* or *bye-bye* mean
(2)   Stop or change direction almost every time when his mother says "No!" or "Stop that!"
(3)   React to indicate that he knows who is being talked about when the name of a family member not in the room is mentioned

(4)   Lift his arms or wave in answer when his mother says words such as "up" or "bye-bye"

(5)   Listen with interest to music or singing and/or move to the beat

(6)   Respond to simple familiar commands such as "Come here!" or "Let's go!"

(7)   Sit still and listen for a full minute to someone who is showing and naming pictures of familiar things (especially in books he likes)

(8)   Enjoy hearing words that name familiar objects

(9)   Say "bye-bye" and "hey" when asked to do so

(10)   Recognize the moods of most speakers (respond to facial expressions)

(11)   Anticipates what is going to happen when familiar routines are announced (especially "Bath time!")

In the area of receptive language, Brandon experienced difficulty with:

(1)   Listening/attending to conversations around him

(2)   Responding to his name being called

(3)   Looking in the direction of a familiar object named

(4)   Following directions to give someone a toy or other object requested

(5)   Following simple directions to "Give me five!" or "Show me your nose."

(6)   Understanding new words each week

(7)   Pointing to objects when named

(8)   Pointing to major body parts named

In the area of Expressive Language, Brandon was reported to:

(1)   Jabber for a long time, talking to toys and people throughout the day

(2)   Frequently respond to songs or rhymes by vocalizing or singing along

(3)   Sometimes produce real words when talking

(4)   Greet and say good-bye to people using the words "hi" and "bye-bye"

(5)   Imitate sounds around him during play such as animal sounds

(6)   Show signs of frustration when he is unable to make others understand him

In the area of expressive language, Brandon was reported to have difficulty with:

(1) Using inflection to ask questions
(2) Combining words with gestures to indicate wants
(3) Repeating or imitating words heard in conversation
(4) Labeling/naming his favorite toys, foods, etc.
(5) Saying at least 50 words
(6) Using any two-word utterances
(7) Producing both the beginning and ending sounds of words

Brandon's mother stated that Brandon has received speech therapy through the Early Steps Program for approximately one year. His mother has seen significant improvements over the past year.

By parent report, Brandon loves to look at books. He wants the same books read to him repeatedly. He will not point to pictures to identify them as his mother reads to him. He taps randomly at pictures he likes. He loves to sing certain songs, especially Ring around the Rosy, Jesus Loves You, Itsy Bitsy Spider, Old McDonald, Rain Rain Go Away, and Row Row Row Your Boat. He also likes watching certain movies and knows the lines from the movie. He will say the movie lines as the movie is playing and also later after the movie is over. He loves to play with his cars (watching the wheels move) and likes to bang his blocks together. Although clapping while watching a ceiling fan used to be an obsession, he no longer exhibits this behavior, but he does flap his hands when he is excited. Brandon does not attend to someone speaking to him for an extended time, but he will attend longer to people with whom he is familiar. His mother also indicated that he rarely follows any directions given to him at home, unless the direction is associated with a familiar routine and is repeated several times. Brandon usually communicates by pulling his mother toward the desired item, and if he cannot make his needs known, he exhibits his frustration through crying or mild fussing. He reportedly says *mama*, *dada*, *ball*, *Cheetos*, *bye-bye*, *ball*, *no*, *yes*, *Mimaw*, *Pawpaw*, and *green*. He will not wave bye-bye, but he will say "bye-bye" appropriately. When asked to imitate a word, Brandon will not give an immediate imitation; rather, he will say the word much later. When he says new words, he does not consistently use the word. He might not readily use the word again. Brandon's mother indicated that Brandon does not have the opportunity to regularly interact with peers. Brandon has a four-year-old brother, Anthony, who he likes to follow around. Brandon interacts with Anthony to sing songs and play ball together.

Observations of Brandon's communication behavior both in the testing environment and in his home environment revealed results consistent with the standardized testing results, indicating significant language delays. Brandon seemed content and mild-mannered during both observations. He carried around a sippy cup with him and sucked and chewed on the soft spout as he walked around, watched television, etc. Brandon's spontaneous vocalizations consisted mostly of strings of unintelligible jargon. The only true words produced were "down" and "no." When Brandon sang or counted, he produced many more words. For example, he sang the entire song Ring around the Rosy by himself. When his mother sang Head, Shoulders, Knees, and Toes, he filled in the appropriate body parts when she stopped singing. Brandon established eye contact with the examiner many times when singing or seeking approval. For example, after stacking a Lego block, he clapped his hands, said "yea," and established eye contact with the examiner. He also evidenced the ability to initiate an interaction or to continue an interaction. After Brandon sang a song several times in a row, the examiner turned around to write a few notes and Brandon tapped her on her back to get her to attend to his singing again. Brandon showed signs of pleasure and a desire to continue back-and-forth interactions with the examiner. As the examiner bumped a truck into Brandon's foot, he laughed heartily and waited expectantly for the examiner to repeat the action. Brandon attended to items/activities of interest for extended periods of time. He allowed his mother to read Ten Little Ladybugs (one of his favorite books) as he sat quietly on her lap and turned each page when she was finished reading. He also allowed his mother to use hand-over-hand prompting to point to the ladybugs in the book without pulling away or refusing to participate. He was not able to independently point to pictures to receptively identify pictures in the book. Brandon did not respond to his name being called by the examiner and he did not readily follow any directions given. He also did not readily respond to vocal models or prompts to encourage verbalizations provided by the examiner.

Brandon's play skills were also observed in his home environment. When Brandon and his brother first began playing with the Lego blocks, Anthony immediately began to build something, while Brandon moved the blocks around and clapped two of them together. When the examiner sat next to Brandon, he began to stack blocks/connect the Legos. Brandon explored each block as he picked it up and did not appear to be aware of the incompatibility that existed with large versus smaller Legos. When he was unable to connect the smaller Lego to the larger one, he placed the smaller Lego in his mouth. He moved the Lego around his mouth without actually chewing or sucking on it. Observation of Brandon's play skills indicated that he is functioning at a pre-symbolic level of play (exploring/sensory level rather than symbolic/pretend play).

Results of speech testing and student observations indicate that Brandon exhibits significant receptive and expressive language delays.

Effect on Educational Performance
Spoken language is an integral part of educational performance. Brandon's communication disorder significantly interferes with his ability to orally communicate what learning processes have been completed and educational concepts mastered. His delay interferes with his ability to comprehend and process oral information presented.

There is a likely potential for change in Brandon's educational functioning if he receives therapeutic intervention.

OCCUPATIONAL THERAPY ASSESSMENT
Brandon was referred for an occupational therapy evaluation due to concerns of possible deficits in his visual motor, fine motor, sensorimotor, and self-help skills that could hinder performance within the educational setting.

The following tests were administered:
(1)   Peabody Developmental Motor Scales-2
(2)   Infant/Toddler Sensory Profile

Brandon's chronological age was 2 years, 8 months. The initial evaluation was unstructured and conducted in a room with minimal distractions at the Special Education office. The second evaluation was unstructured and conducted at Brandon's home. In addition to administered tests, a review of Brandon's file, conversations with his parent, clinical observations, and task performance observations were made.

Brandon accepted the examiner with some difficulty. Brandon was nonverbal, but communicated with gestures.

Brandon had appropriate eye contact at times and then avoided eye contact at other times. He showed tactile defensive responses such as hand flapping, toe-walking, rocking on furniture, and leaning on large objects. Brandon did not cooperate at all times, making it difficult to determine if he could not or would not perform the tasks. His attention span was short in a one-to-one situation. He was unable to follow directions given.

Clinical Observations
Primitive reflexes appeared integrated. Equilibrium and protective extension reactions were present. Muscle tone and joint range of motion were within normal limits throughout the trunk and upper extremities. Muscle strength is adequate for functional activities.

Difficulty with postural stability might contribute to difficulty performing both gross and fine motor tasks.

Brandon's motor planning skills were poor based on the examiner's clinical observations.

Throughout testing, Brandon exhibited no problems crossing the vertical body midline with his hands during fine motor and gross motor tasks.

Brandon was observed walking in a repetitious pattern along lined furniture at times. He also walked in a repetitious pattern perpendicular to lined furniture and would look at the lined furniture through his peripheral vision as he passed the furniture. He flapped his hands while watching television and while looking at lined furniture. He was very active. He touched and manipulated blocks, but did not play with them correctly initially until a speech therapist showed him. He then needed constant cuing and much praise to continue to play with the blocks. He parallel played with his brother. He drank from a sippy-cup and sucked from it, at times with no liquid coming out. He does not point to objects. Brandon is able to control some of the behaviors he performs by verbal or tactile cues from his mother.

Sensory

The Infant/Toddler Sensory Profile was administered. The profile provides a standard method to measure a child's sensory processing abilities. The profile looks at the effects of sensory processing on the child's functional performance in daily life, provides information about the child's tendencies to respond to stimuli, and which sensory systems are likely to be contributing to or creating barriers to functional performance.

The Infant/Toddler Sensory Profile is a judgement-based professional/caregiver questionnaire. It consists of 48 items for children 7 to 36 months of age. There are five sensory processing section scores, four quadrant scores, and one combined quadrant score available. The quadrant scores reflect the child's responsiveness to sensory experiences. Sensation Seeking and Low Registration indicate different *high* threshold responses, while Sensory Sensitivity and Sensation Avoiding reflect different *low* threshold responses. There is also a combined quadrant score (Low Threshold) that is the combination of Sensory Sensitivity and Sensation Avoiding quadrant scores.

INFANT / TODDLER SENSORY PROFILE

	QUADRANT RAW SCORE TOTAL	MORE / LESS THAN OTHERS
Low Registration	38/55	More Definite
Sensation Seeking	31/70	Typical Performance
Sensation Sensitivity	43/55	Typical Performance
Sensation Avoiding	37/60	More Definite
Low Threshold	80/115	More Probable

Brandon has sensory processing problems with responding to situation and people, avoiding situations and people, and oral sensory processing.

Brandon has questionable sensory processing problems with change in schedule and situations, auditory processing, and vestibular processing.

Typical Performance includes scores at or above 1 standard deviation below the mean. This range indicates the child performs in the top 84 percent of children without disabilities.

Probable Performance includes scores between 1 and 2 standard deviations below the mean. Scores that fall within the range indicate sensory processing abilities are questionable in these areas. This range indicates the child performs between the 2nd and 84th percentile of children without disabilities.

Definite Performance includes scores 2 standard deviations below the mean. Scores that fall within this range indicate sensory processing problems. This range indicates the child performs in the lowest 2 percent of children without disabilities.

Fine Motor and Visual Motor

The Fine Motor Scale of the Peabody Developmental Motor Scales-2 was administered. This is an individually administered standardized test that measures the fine motor skills of children from birth through 6 years. The fine motor scale consists of tasks that require precise movement of the small muscles of the body. The items are classified into skill categories of grasping and visual motor integration. The Peabody Developmental Motor Scales-2 was unable to be completed due to Brandon's poor direction following skills, sensory processing problems, and poor participation. It was unclear if Brandon has developed a hand preference. He refused to hold a marker to scribble.

Self-Help

Brandon's self-help skills were assessed through consultation with his mother. He requires assistance with dressing and feeding skills. He refuses to feed himself with a spoon and refuses to be fed with a spoon. He only eats finger foods. He is not potty trained.

Strengths and Weaknesses

The occupational therapist found relative strengths in Brandon's:

(1) Bilateral motor coordination
(2) Functional grasp, release, and manipulation of objects
(3) Joint range of motion
(4) Muscle strength and endurance
(5) Muscle tone
(6) Oral motor function
(7) Family support
(8) Some behaviors manageable

Relative weaknesses were found by the occupational therapist in Brandon's:

(1) Short attention span
(2) Lack of cooperation in testing situation
(3) Ability to follow multiple directions
(4) Undeveloped hand preference
(5) Motor planning
(6) Fine motor skills
(7) Visual-motor coordination
(8) Visual perception
(9) Sensory processing
(10) Self-care
(11) Pre-handwriting skills

A review of this occupational therapy evaluation data indicates that Brandon exhibits an inability to integrate sensory stimuli, thereby affecting his ability to perform functional activities within the educational setting. These deficits in sensory integration contribute to delays in fine motor, visual motor, and self-help skills.

These deficits interfere with Brandon's ability to benefit from his educational program. In addition to occupational therapy assessment, current student information indicates that the ability to improve functional activity performance through occupational therapy intervention is present.

Based upon these considerations and on evaluation data, Brandon met eligibility criteria and, therefore, does appear to demonstrate or exhibit a need for intervention in the area of occupational therapy to benefit from his special education program.

PSYCHOLOGICAL ASSESSMENT
Behavioral Observation
Observation of Brandon with his mother in the testing environment (at the Special Education building) and his mother and brother in the home environment were conducted.

At the Special Education building, it was noted that Brandon appeared aware of his surroundings and things happening in his environment. Although he did not establish or maintain eye contact, he appeared aware of events occurring in the room. For example, as the examiner took out toys, Brandon would come to the table to look at or manipulate the object, if he was interested. He did not come to the table and could not be redirected to the table for all items presented. During the evaluation session, Brandon walked on the side of a row of tables or walked down a straight line looking back out of the corner of his eye. When getting to the end of the table or line, Brandon would excitedly flap his hands. He carried a sippy cup with him throughout most of the observation period. This cup appeared to serve as a security for Brandon more than a means to obtain liquid. He rarely sipped on the cup, but mostly chewed on the soft tip. Brandon did not respond to verbal requests made by the examiners. He did not turn or look toward the examiner when his name was called. He did respond to his mother when repeated verbal requests were made.

In the home setting, Brandon appeared more comfortable and at ease. He watched a television show, intermittently flapping his hands when he became excited. He interacted with his brother by performing an action and looking toward his brother who usually imitated the action. He appeared to enjoy this interaction. He also enjoyed hearing a book read by his mother. Brandon did not respond to his name being called by the observer, but did interact with the speech therapist while playing with blocks. He did respond to requests made by his mother.

Gilliam Autism Rating Scale

Autistic behaviors were further assessed in the home setting utilizing the Gilliam Autism Rating Scale (GARS). The GARS is a behavioral checklist that helps identify persons who are autistic. It is comprised of four subtests which include Stereotyped Behaviors, Communication, Social Interaction, and Development. Each subtest is comprised of 14 items describing behaviors that are symptomatic of autism.

The first subtest, Stereotyped Behaviors, describes stereotyped behaviors, motility disorders, and other unique and strange behaviors. Communication, the second subtest, describes verbal and nonverbal behaviors that are symptomatic of autism. Social Interaction is the third subtest and evaluates the person's ability to relate appropriately to people, events, and objects. The final subtest, Developmental Disturbances, asks key questions about the subject's development during early childhood.

By comparing Brandon's scores with the normative sample, which was composed entirely of individuals diagnosed as autistic, the probability of autism can be estimated. The best overall estimate of a subject's behavior is the Autism Quotient. This standard score takes into account all the symptomatic behavior of autism measured on the GARS. Autism Quotients of 80 through 89 are below average for subjects with autism and represent borderline scores in terms of the likelihood of autism. If the Autism Quotient is 90 or above, the person is probably autistic. Autism Quotients of 90 through 110 are within the average range for subjects with autism in the normative sample. Autism Quotients equal to or greater than 111 are highly indicative of autism.

Results of the GARS administered to Brandon's mother were as follows:
GILLIAM AUTISM RATING SCALE (Parent)

	PERCENTILE	STANDARD SCORE	PROBABILITY OF AUTISM
Stereotyped Behaviors	25	8	Average
Communication	50	10	Average
Social Interaction	1	3	Very Low
Developmental	16	7	Below Average
AUTISM QUOTIENT	9	80	Below Average

The results obtained from the GARS revealed an Autism Quotient of 80 indicating that Brandon's probability of autism is Below Average.

INTEGRATED SUMMARY OF FINDINGS

A developmental assessment was conducted. Brandon is functioning significantly below age expectancy in the areas of physical development; social, adaptive or emotional development; and cognitive and communication development.

The effects of the impairment or condition on Brandon's educational performance in the appropriate developmental activities include possible difficulties with the following:

    (1)   Progress at the same rate as age peers

    (2)   Become increasingly more independent with self-care skills

    (3)   Work independently

    (4)   Communicate learning processes completed and educational concepts mastered

    (5)   Development of self-concept, peer interactions, coping skills, and social growth

    (6)   Perform tasks involving reasoning and academic skills, memory, perceptual discrimination, and concept development

    (7)   Perform tasks requiring fine motor skills

    (8)   Attend to, process, and respond to sensory input from his environment

Results of this evaluation reveal that Brandon meets the criteria for classification of **DEVELOPMENTAL DELAY** as determined by Louisiana Bulletin 1508. Brandon qualifies to receive **speech/language pathology services** and **occupational therapy** services.

It is the opinion of this evaluation coordinator and the multidisciplinary team that the following factors did not interfere with the reliability of the evaluation data: communication barrier, environmental conditions, rapport, motivation, length of examination, race, culture, and sex. No discrepancies were noted.

EDUCATIONAL NEEDS AND RECOMMENDATIONS
FOR
BRANDON

COMMUNICATION NEEDS

(1) <u>Language</u> - Brandon would benefit from speech/language pathology services/classroom interventions to improve his receptive and expressive language skills. IEP goals and objectives should focus on those language skills which most significantly impact Brandon's educational performance. Consideration should be given to the language arts curriculum standards at or below his grade level which have not been achieved. Materials and resources from Brandon's classroom should be incorporated into his therapy program.

(2) The therapist might want to consider addressing some of the following language objectives during therapy sessions:

    (A) Receptively identifying basic pictures in books or three-dimensional items.

    (B) Using a picture exchange system to enhance communicative abilities.

    (C) Following simple directions with cues/models.

    (D) Following a basic picture schedule (to assist with transitions from one activity to the next).

    (E) Facilitating appropriate symbolic play.

    (F) Attending to someone speaking for at least 10 seconds with minimal redirection.

    (G) Attending to a variety of storybooks.

    (H) Increasing his expressive vocabulary skills.

    (I) Initiating interaction with peers and teachers (by setting up communicative temptations).

(3)   If the therapist has difficulty establishing rapport with Brandon or making Brandon feel comfortable with the therapy/classroom environment, she might want to try allowing him to bring his sippy cup into the therapy session to make him feel more comfortable. She could also attempt to sing some of his favorite songs with him or have Brandon's mother send some of his favorite books with him to school to utilize in therapy sessions.

(4)   <u>Articulation</u> - Brandon's articulation skills should be monitored as his expressive language skills develop.

EDUCATIONAL NEEDS

(1)   Brandon should be provided with the opportunity to further develop cognitive skills. He should be taught using a developmental curriculum. Skills not yet achieved, such as those listed in the Cognitive subtest of the BDI-2, should be the focus of IEP goals and objectives. Specific areas of concern include attention and memory; perception and concepts; visually and auditorily attend to environmental stimuli for varying lengths of time; perceive, identify, and solve problems; and analyze and appraise the elements of situations.

(2)   Brandon should be provided with guided opportunities to develop personal-social skills that will allow him to engage in meaningful social interactions with adults and peers. Skills such as those listed in this report should be the focus of IEP goals and objectives. He should be taught using a developmental curriculum. Specific areas of concern include respond to and initiate social contacts with peers and interact effectively in a small group.

(3)   Adaptive (self-help) skills should be taught using a developmental curriculum. Skills not yet achieved, such as those listed in the Adapted subtest of the BDI-2, should be the focus of IEP goals and objectives. Of particular concern are the areas of eating, dressing, and toileting.

(4)   Fine Motor skills should be taught using a developmental curriculum. Skills not yet achieved, listed in the Fine Motor subtest of the BDI-2, should be the focus of IEP goals and objectives. Also:

    (A)   Classroom activities be organized with a visual schedule.

    (B)   Perform activities with Play-Doh, sand, beans, rice, pudding, and other multisensory items when performing prehandwriting activities.

    (C)   Give boundaries for sitting activities (tape, carpet squares, etc.).

    (D)   Perform cutting activities.

    (E)   Perform block/Lego activities.

    (F)   Give fidget toys.

    (G)   Teach him to run, spin, push toys, and/or ride bikes at recess.

    (H)   Allow him to use plasticware to feed himself.

    (I)   Allow him to go in a tent or relax on a beanbag, when needed.

(2)   The following activities are suggested recommendation to improve socialization and participation in the area of gross motor:

    (A)   Participation in small group activities.

    (B)   Stay at a task.

    (C)   Listen and follow teacher instructions.

STUDENT'S NAME: Brandon

A. DIAGNOSED IMPAIRMENT OR CONDITION: Delays in Personal-Social, Adaptive,
Fine Motor, Perceptual Motor,
Receptive Communication,
Expressive Communication,
Cognitive; Articulation Development

B. NEED FOR SPECIAL EDUCATION: Yes

C. PRIMARY EXCEPTIONALITY: **DEVELOPMENTAL DELAY**

D. OTHER SERVICES NEEDED: Occupational Therapy
Speech/Language Pathology Services

We certify that this report represents the best, integrated description of this student at this time.
The evaluation meets the criteria for eligibility and required evaluation procedures for the
exceptionality listed above

_____
EVALUATION COORDINATOR
CERTIFIED SCHOOL SOCIAL WORKER
Patricia

_____
ADAPTED PHYSICAL EDUCATION TEACHER
Angela

_____
CERTIFIED SCHOOL PSYCHOLOGIST
Ellen

_____
SPEECH/LANGUAGE PATHOLOGIST
Mandy

_____
OCCUPATIONAL THERAPIST
Jenie

_____
SPECIAL EDUCATION NURSE
Jimmie

TYPIST: PAP/mas

Page 26 of 26

APPENDIX C

2008 ATLANTA, DEKALB COUNTY, GEORGIA SCHOOLS

DeKalb County School System, Georgia
PARENT NOTIFICATION

Student Name		randon	
	(last)	(first)	(middle)

Dear Mrs.

There will be a meeting to discuss your child's educational program. All pertinent information will be reviewed so that the committee may determine an appropriate educational program in the least restrictive educational setting. If eligibility for special education services is determined, an Individualized Education Program (IEP) will be developed. Placement recommendations will be based on the IEP.

Purpose of Meeting:

- [ ] Discuss evaluation results and determine eligibility
- [ ] Develop an Individualized Education Program (IEP)
- [ ] Review current IEP
- [ ] Amend current IEP
- [ ] Develop IEP for the next school year
- [ ] Develop/Revise Behavior Intervention Plan
- [ ] Other:

- [ ] Discuss disciplinary action/discipline review
- [ ] Develop Transition Plan
- [ ] Discuss re-evaluation results/re-evaluation consideration
- [ ] Discuss new information and consider appropriate program changes
- [x] Interim IEP

Date: 8/28/07	Location: Idlewood Elem.	Time: 1:15

The following persons have been invited to this meeting:

Name	Title	Name	Title
	General Education Teacher		
Nichole	Special Education Teacher		
	Administrator		
	Student*		
Kymberly	LTSE		

STUDENTS 14 YEARS AND OLDER MUST BE INVITED FOR TRANSITION PLANNING. ALL 18-YEAR-OLD STUDENTS MUST BE INVITED TO IEP MEETINGS.

[ ] Parent contacted by phone: 8/27/07	[ ] Student contacted (when appropriate):
(date)	(date)

Your attendance is important, although not required. Your presence will be helpful in planning for your child's educational needs. If the time or date is not convenient, please contact me so that I can reschedule this conference. You may invite anyone you wish. Please let me know if you will be inviting anyone so that I can arrange for an appropriate meeting space. If you have questions, please contact me at _____.

Sincerely,

Name: Kymberly	Chairperson
Title: LTSE	Date: 8/14/07

Indicate if you will be able to attend by checking the appropriate box below. Please sign and return this form.

- [x] Yes, I will attend.
- [ ] I cannot attend the meeting at the suggested time. Please contact me to reschedule.
- [ ] No, I will not be attending the meeting, but I understand a copy of the recommendations will be sent to me.

Parent/Guardian/Surrogate/Student Signature	8/28/07
	Date

STAFFING COMMITTEE MEETING AND INDIVIDUALIZED EDUCATION PROGRAM (IEP)
DEPARTMENT OF EXCEPTIONAL EDUCATION AND SUPPORT SERVICES. DEKALB COUNTY SCHOOL SYSTEM, GEORGIA

☐ INITIAL ☐ REVIEW ☒ INTERIM ☐ MOVE-IN

| Name: | Brandon | | Student #: | | Date of Birth: | | Date: | 8/28/07 |
| | (last) | (first) | (middle) | | | | | |

Home School:

Current School:

Physical/Medical Limitations:

Current Grade: pre-k

Primary Area of Disability: Significant Developmental Delay (SDD)   Other Disability(ies): Speech Impaired

Related Service: occupational therapy

Present Levels of Performance
Strengths/weaknesses of student:

According to Terrebonne Parish Public Schools, in the area of adaptive skills, Brandon is able to feed himself bite-sized pieces of food, ask for food or liquid with words or gestures, and help dress by holding out his arms or legs. He refuses to drink from a cup or glass but he is able to drink from a sippy cup. He does not respond, accurately, yes or no when he is asked if he needs to use the restroom.

They report that in the area of personal-social he is responsive to adult praise, adult greetings(familiar adults), rewards, and the promise of rewards. He has been observed playing with others during small group time. He did not demonstrate the ability to state his first name or identify himself in a mirror.

Terrebonne Parish also documented that, in the area of motor skills, Brandon is able to scribble on paper, maintain or correct his balance when transitioning from standing to non-vertical positions. He is able to walk up and down stairs without assistance. Brandon wasn't able to run 10 feet or kick a ball forward without falling.

They report that in the area of cognitive development, Brandon is able to attend to an activity for 3 or more minutes, occupy himself for 10 or more minutes, and point to or touch pictures in a book. He wasn't observed responding to one and one more, search for a removed object, or match colors.

In the area of communication, it is noted that he has significant expressive and receptive language delays. He has difficulty repeating or imitating words or gestures, labeling/naming items of interest, listening/attending to a conversation around him, expressing his wants and needs, directing attention to himself, and greeting familiar adults/peers.

Parental input:

Brandon will not eat with a fork or spoon. Will respond to it's time to Poddy. Taken once every hour or every half hour. He does repeat single words and phrases.

Current functioning, including specific information on literacy and numeracy skills, as appropriate:

Student is served in the pre-k 4 class. According to Terrebonne Parish Public Schools, Brandon is able to point to pictures in books but he is unable to match colors. He does not state his first name and he does not indicate the understanding of "one more". He also knows the primary colors

Impact of disability on progress in general curriculum and nonacademic areas (if preschool, impact on participation in appropriate activities):

Brandon's disability impacts his ability to communicate and socialize with his peers and adults.

Date(s) and results of initial or most recent evaluation(s):

| 10/24/05 Battelle Developmental Inventory, 2nd Edition: Adaptive – 73, Personal-Social – 77, Motor – 70, Cognitive - 68 | 10/24/05 – BDI-2: Total communication 55 (receptive = 7 months, expressive = 8 months) | 10/24/05 – Receptive-Expressive Emergent Language Test-Third Edition (REEL-3): Receptive – 56, Expressive – 63, Language Ability Score - 51 |

| Disabilities: | (a) SDD | ER Date: none on file | (c) OT | ER Date: none on file |
| | (b) SI | ER Date: none on file | (d) | ER Date: |

Results of state-wide or district-wide assessments:

Student is pre-k – none on file

DeKalb County School System

Revised August 1, 2006

Name:		Student #:	Disability(ies): SDD, SI, OT	Date: 8/28/07
Brandon				
(last)	_(first)_			

Special Factors

Does the student have behavior which impedes his/her learning or the learning of others?

☐ yes

If yes, attach a Behavioral Intervention Plan which includes positive interventions, strategies, consequences, and supports to address the behavior.

☒ no

Does the student have limited English proficiency? *If yes, describe the language needs as related to the IEP.*

☐ yes

☒ no

Is the student blind or visually impaired? *If yes, provide for instruction in Braille and the use of Braille, unless the IEP Team determines that instruction in Braille is not appropriate for the student. Document decisions below.*

☐ yes

☒ no

Is the student deaf or hard of hearing? *If yes, describe below the student's language and communication needs, opportunities for direct communications with peers and professional personnel in the student's language and communication mode, academic level and full range of needs, including opportunities for direct instruction in the student's language and communication mode.*

☐ yes

☒ no

Assistive technology has been considered. *Check one of the following.*

☒ Educationally essential tasks **can be** accomplished with standard classroom tools. Assistive technology **is not** required.

☐ Student is currently using assistive technology as described in Present Levels of Performance on page 1 of the IEP.

☐ Refer for assistive technology evaluation.

Does the student have communication needs which have not been addressed in this IEP? *If yes, describe below.*

☐ yes

☒ no

Name: _____, Brandon _____

(last) (first) (middle)

Student #: _____

Disability(ies): SDD, SI, OT

Date: 8/28/07

Goals and Objectives

Annual Goals and Short-Term Behavioral Objectives	Method	Person	Current Status %	Performance Data													Projected Performance	
				Date	Status %	Date	Status %	Date	Status %	Date	Status %	Date	Status %	Date	Status %	Date	Status %
Increase adaptive skills																	
a. drink from a cup without assistance and with little spilling	DC	SET															75%
b. ask for food or liquid with words or gestures	DC	SET															75%
c. express a need to use the toilet	DC	SET															75%
Increase personal-social skills																	
a. identify self in mirror	DC	SET															75%
b. state first name	DC	SET															75%
c. use objects in make-believe play	DC	SET															75%
Increase motor skills																	
a. propel or throw an object	DC	OT / SET															75%
b. grasp crayon using pads of fingertips	DC	OT / SET															75%
c. place 4 rings on a post in any order	DC	OT / SET															75%
Increase cognitive skills																	
a. search for a removed object	DC	SET															75%
b. nest objects inside one another	DC	SET															75%
c. match colors	DC	SET															75%
d. respond to one or one more	DC	SET															75%

The student's progress toward annual goals will be reported to parents on the same schedule as students in general education.

Key
SET = Special Education Teacher
GET = General Education Teacher
SLP = Speech/Language Pathologist

OT = Occupational Therapist
PT = Physical Therapist
TVI = Teacher, Visually Impaired

DC = Data Collection
SR = Severe Regression
* = Graduation

IA = Informal Assessment
GAA = Georgia Alternate Assessment

DeKalb County School System

Revised August 1, 2006

CONFIDENTIAL

Name: _____ Brandon _____ Student #: _____ Disability(ies): SDD, SI, OT Date: 8/28/07
(last) (first) (middle)

Goals and Objectives

Annual Goals and Short-Term Behavioral Objectives	Method	Person	Current Status %	Criteria Date	Performance Data												Projected Performance		
					Status %	Date	Status %	Date	Status %	Date	Status %	Date	Status %	Date		Date	Status %
Increase expressive and receptive language																			
a. label items of interest using pictures, gestures, or verbal responses	DC	SI / SET															70%
b. request wants and needs using pictures, gestures, or verbal responses	DC	SI / SET															70%
c. greet familiar adults/peers using gestures or verbal response	DC	SI / SET															70%
d. repeat/imitate words or gestures	DC	SI / SET															70%

The student's progress toward annual goals will be reported to parents on the same schedule as students in general education.

Name				Student #:		Disability(ies): SDD, SI, OT		Date: 8/28/07
	Brandon							
(last)	(first)	(middle)						

Start Date: 8/28/07   End Date: Oct 5, 2004

Classroom/Program Modifications

Modifications Needed for the Student:
(To advance appropriately toward attaining the annual goals; to be involved and progress in the general curriculum; to participate in extracurricular and other nonacademic activities; to be educated and participate with other students with and without disabilities.)

A.   Supplementary Aids and Services:

~~Picture exchange~~
none

B.   Instructional Modifications or Supports for School Personnel:

C.   Grading Modifications:

D.   Modifications for Participation in Extracurricular Activities/Other Nonacademic Activities:

Brandon _____ will participate in extracurricular/nonacademic activities according to the same guidelines as non-disabled peers

E.   Other Modifications Needed:

Distribute copies of this page to all teachers who will be implementing the IEP.

DeKalb County School System   Revised August 1, 2006

CONFIDENTIAL

Name:				Student #:		
	(last)	(first)	(middle)		Disability(ies): SDD, SI, OT	Date: 8/28/07

Current Grade: Pre-k (4) (07-08)	Projected Grade: kindergarten (08-09)

Test Participation

1. ☒ No state or system-wide testing is conducted for 3- and 4-year-old students or students in grade 9, 10, and 12 who are working toward a Transition Diploma.

2. ☐ Student will participate in state or system-wide standardized testing.

State of Georgia Tests:

☐ Georgia Kindergarten Assessment Program (GKAP)
☐ Curriculum-Based Assessment-Writing Test (CBAWT) – 3, 5, 8
☐ Criterion Referenced Competency Test (CRCT) – 1, 2, 3, 4, 5, 6, 7, 8
☐ Georgia High School Graduation Test (GHSGT) – 11 (no alternate assessment)
☐ Georgia High School Graduation Writing Test (GHSWT) – 11 (no alternate assessment)
☐ End of Course Test

System-Wide Tests:

☐ Cognitive Abilities Test (COGAT) – 1, 3, 5, 7
☐ Future Focus (FF) – 6
☐ Renzulli – 1, 3, 5, 7
☐ Norm-referenced Test
☐ Other
☐ Other

Describe the accommodations the student needs in order to participate.
Accommodations used for assessment must be consistent with accommodations used for classroom instruction and specified in the IEP.

Test	Setting	Timing/Scheduling	Presentation	Response	Standard/Nonstandard	
					S ☐	NS ☐
					S ☐	NS ☐
					S ☐	NS ☐
					S ☐	NS ☐
					S ☐	NS ☐

3. ☐ Student will not participate in COGAT. Individual cognitive assessment is on file.

4. ☐ This is to inform you that the Georgia Academic Promotion Placement and Retention Law requires that all 3rd, 5th, and 8th grade students pass the required sections of the CRCT in order to be promoted to the next grade. (O.C.G.A. 20-2-282 through 20-2-285).

5. ☐ This is to inform you that students are required to pass all portions of the Georgia High School Graduation Test in order to receive a General Education High School Diploma (O.C.G.A. 20-2-281).

6. ☐ Student will participate in the Georgia Alternate Assessment (GAA). Even with maximum accommodations, the student cannot participate in a group test. All grade appropriate general education curricular areas will be assessed through alternative achievement standards in the form of an individual portfolio assessment.

Name: _____

(la...) (first) (middle)   Student #: _____   Disability(ies): SDD, SI, OT   Date: 8/28/07

Placement Recommendations

☐	1. General education setting only
☐	2. General education setting with consultative services
☐	3. General education setting with supplemental aids and services
☐	4. General education setting with direct speech/language therapy services
☐	5. General education setting with direct special education **half day or less**
☐	6. General education setting with direct special education **more than half** day
☒	7. Self-contained setting with participation with non-disabled students for:
☒	8. Self-contained setting
☒	9. Separate school/center
☒	10. Community-based services
☒	11. Related Services (specify): speech impaired, occupational therapy
☐	12. Other:

Options Rejected

9,10	Does not provide the type or intensity of support and related services necessary to address the goals and objectives to the maximum extent appropriate.
9,10	Does not provide specialized instructional intervention and/or modifications to address goals and objectives to the maximum extent appropriate.
9,10	Does not provide the amount of Individual or small group instruction required to address student's educational needs.
9,10	Does not provide appropriate educational services in the least restrictive environment.
	Other Rationale:

Placement option(s) recommended/accepted and rationale for final decisions:
(Include an explanation of the extent, if any, to which the student will not participate with non-disabled peers.) 11

Option 8 was selected to address Brandon's goals and objectives in a small group setting with his peers. Option 4 was selected to address deficits in the areas of speech and fine motor.

The IEP committee has reviewed this IEP with respect to the continuum of placement options and has determined that this placement is the least restrictive environment in which the goals and objectives can be implemented.

IEP Committee:

Name	Position/Title	Name	Position/Title
	Parent *(if present in meeting)*		
	SS Representative	usp	Speech-Language Pathologist
	General Education Teacher		
	Special Education Teacher		

DeKalb County School System   Revised August 1, 2006

Name			Student #:		Disability(ies): SDD, SI, OT	Date: 8/28/07
	Brandon					
(last)	(first)	(middle)				

Special Education (SE)/Related Services/Supplementary Aids and Services	Location GE/SE	Amount of Time Weekly	Projected Duration (Excluding Summer Months)	
			Begin (M/D/Y)	End (M/D/Y)
SDD	SE	28.75	8/28/07	10/5/07
OT	SE	.25	8/28/07	10/5/07
SI	SE	1.0	8/28/07	10/5/07
General Education (GE)	GE	0		
General Education (GE)	GE			

Physical Education: ☐ Regular ☐ Adapted ☒ Not Required	Transition Plan (Required for students 14 and older) Attached: ☐ Yes ☒ N/A
Special Transportation: ☒ Yes ☐ No	Proposed Servicing School: Idlewood
Transportation Adaptations: CRS	Proposed Grade: pre-k (07-08), k (08-09)
Case Manager: N. Edwards	Annual Review Date: 8/27/08

Name: _____ , Brandon _____

(last) *(first)* *(middle)*

Student #: _____

Disability(ies): SDD, SI, OT   Date: 8/28/07

Extended School Year

Discuss extended school year at the annual review and check one of three statements below:

☐ Based on a review of pertinent educational information, an extended school year program **is not** recommended. Any committee member may request an IEP review prior to the end of the school year to reconsider the need for ESY. _____ *(date).*

☐ Based on a review of pertinent educational information, an extended school year program **is** recommended. *(Attach ESY Addendum).* _____ *(date).*

☒ Based on a review of pertinent educational information, an extended school year program cannot be determined at this time. An IEP meeting will be convened to make a recommendation concerning the need for an extended school year program after the spring break. ___8/28/07___ _____ *(date).*

Parent Contacts and Notice Regarding this IEP

Date	Method	Result	Date	Method	Result
8/27/07	Phone call	Parent stated that she could attend			
8/28/07		Parents attended			

Prior Notice of Actions Proposed/Refused

Did the parent/guardian/surrogate attend the IEP meeting?

☒ **Yes.** *Complete signature section below.*

This is to certify that I was invited to participate in the development of the IEP and understand its contents. I have had explained to me the due process rights and procedures. I have received a copy of the following: *(Check as appropriate)*

☒ "Your Rights as Parents Regarding Special Education"   ☒ IEP   ☐ Eligibility Report(s)   ☐ Evaluation Report(s)

Signature: _____   Date: ___8/28/08___

Parent/Guardian/Surrogate

☐ **No.** *Indicate the date copies were mailed/sent to the parent/guardian/surrogate to serve as notice of actions proposed or refused.* *(Check as appropriate)*
Date mailed/sent: _____

☐ "Your Rights as Parents Regarding Special Education"   ☐ IEP   ☐ Eligibility Report(s)   ☐ Evaluation Report(s)

For Initial Placement Only

Parental Consent for Placement

After considering my child's present levels of performance and pertinent information, I am in agreement with the recommendations for special education and related services as proposed in this I

Signature: _____   Date: ___8/28/08___

Parent/Guardian/Surrogate

DeKalb County School System

Revised August 1, 2006

CONFIDENTIAL

Name:

	Student #:	Date of Birth:	
Brandon			Date:
(last) (first) (middle)			

to well to OT. Brandon will participate in extracurricular non academic activities according to the same guidelines as non-disabled peers. 30 day will be up on October 5, 2014. Brandon will receive SDD 28.75, OT 0.25 and Speech for 1 hour. Brandon will attend school 14-F. Brandon's parents received a PCE form for an evaluation. Parents completed transportation form. Copies were made and distributed and the meeting was adjourned.

IEP Committee Members Present:

Name	Position/Title	Name	Position/Title

UPDATED ELIGIBILITY INFORMATION

☐ DISCIPLINE IEP

Name				Student	Date of Birth:	Date: August 2004
(last)	(first) Brandon	(middle)				

The purpose of this meeting is for Brandon. Mom stated that Brandon was potty trained. A copy of Yu Puerto Rights was given or explained to the parents. Copies of these will give to Brandon's movements for trusing for Brandon.

Won't eat from a fork or spoon, puts finger food mostly. Brandon won't tell you that he has to potty, but will go if you say let's potty. Brandon plays with others but does not play. His attention span is to that focus. Brandon is able to attend to an activity for 10 or more minutes. Brandon has problems expressing his wants and needs. Brandon needs one on one to help him focus. Ms.

Brandon does know his numbers + colors. Brandon is SSB local. Assistive technology is not needed at this time. Ms. Trevino reviewed Brandon's IEP. Brandon will also receive speech

IEP Committee Members Present:

Name	Position/Title
see page 1 for signatures	

Name	Position/Title

DeKalb County School System

Revised August 2, 2006

CONFIDENTIAL

083
027

Parental Consent for Evaluation (PCE)

☒ Initial
☐ Re-evaluation

Date: 8/28/07

Dear Parent/Legal Guardian/Surrogate Parent of _____ Brandon _____
(Last Name, First Name Middle Name)

Your child was referred by _____ Mrs. _____ and was recommended for evaluation by the
(Name)   (Title)
Student Support Team or other appropriate source. We would like to arrange for an individual evaluation to gather more information about how to better meet your child's needs.

If you have any questions about why your child needs testing or want to know more details about the evaluation, please call _____ _____ at __ ·· _____ .
(Name / Title)   (Phone Number)
If you agree to have this evaluation done, you can request to know the time and place that it will occur. You will have a chance to discuss the results within 30 school days following the evaluation. You will also be invited to a meeting to discuss the findings. No changes will be made in your child's educational program until we hold the meeting.

The individual evaluation may include tests in the following areas: vision, hearing, motor skills, intellectual, social/emotional, achievement, speech/language or others. An explanation of these areas is included. A copy of your parents' rights regarding consent and evaluation procedures are attached.

Please sign below to let us know whether or not you agree for testing to take place and return this letter to _____ . If you do not return this form within two weeks, we will contact you about your
(Name)
decision.

Thank you for your cooperation.

Sincerely,

_____   _____   ____LTSE____   _____
(Name)   (Title)   (Phone)

I have read or had read to me the parents' rights provided with this document. The box checked below indicates my decision.

☒ Yes, I agree for the DeKalb County School System to evaluate my child.
☐ No, I do not agree with the recommendation.

_____   _____ 8/28/07 _____
(Signature of Parent/Guardian/Surrogate)   (Date)

Address __

Phone (H) _____

Phone (W) _____

For School Use Only	
Date Received by SST Chairperson:	Date Received by Special Education Dept:

DeKalb County School System   Revised September 19, 2005   CONFIDENTIAL

The purpose of the following evaluations is to determine individual educational needs and may result in a recommendation for special education placement or services. Test(s) will be administered to your child in the area(s) that have been checked.

☒ **VISION** (To be administered by trained personnel)
Purpose: These screening instruments determine the child's visual acuity. If additional testing is indicated, the child may be referred to a medical specialist. Tests may include, but are not limited to: Smellen, Broken Wheel Test of Visual Acuity, Washer Visual Acuity Screening.

☒ **HEARING** (To be administered by trained personnel)
Purpose: These screening and diagnostic instruments determine the child's hearing acuity and functional hearing. If additional testing is indicated, the child may be referred to an audiologist or medical specialist. Tests may include, but are not limited to: air and bone conduction pure-tone audiometry, speech awareness, reception, impedance audiometry and visual inspection of the external ear.

☐ **PSYCHOLOGICAL** (To be administered by a psychologist)
Purpose: Tests used during pschoeducational assessment usually include instruments which measure a child's general intelligence, fine motor skills, emotional/behavioral functioning, and achievement levels. Tests may include, but are not limited to: Wechsler Intelligence Scales (WISC-III, WPPSI-R, WAIS-R), Stanford-Binet Intelligence Scales, Arthur Adaptation-Leiter International Performance Scale, Kaufman Brief Intelligence Test, Kaufman Assessment Battery for Children, Cattell Intelligence Scale, Wechsler Individual Achievement Test, Bender-Gestalt Visual-Motor Integration Test, interviews and observations, and/or self-concept measures.

☐ **ACHIEVEMENT/EDUCATIONAL** (To be administered by trained special education personnel)
Purpose: These group or individual tests determine the child's current level of academic/educational functioning. Tests may include, but are not limited to: Peabody Individual Achievement Test-Revised, Brigance Inventory of Basic Skills, Woodcock Johnson-Revised Test of Achievement, Kaufman-Test of Educational Achievement, Diagnostic Achievement Battery-2, Beery Developmental Test of Visual Motor Integration, Motor-Free Perception Test, Early Screening Profile, Battelle Developmental Inventory, informal assessments, and observations.

☒ **SPEECH/LANGUAGE** (To be administered by a speech pathologist)
Purpose: These tests measure the child's ability to understand, relate to and use language and speech appropriately. Tests may include, but are not limited to: Goldman-Fristoe Test of Articulation, Language Processing Test-Revised, Test of Problem Solving, The Listening Test, Test of Word Knowledge, Evaluating Acquired Skills in Communication-Revised, informal assessments, and observations.

☐ **BEHAVIORAL** (To be administered by trained special education personnel)
Purpose: These tests assess the child's ability to act and interact appropriately in everyday situations with the school and family. Tests may include, but are not limited to: Coopersmith Self-Esteem Inventory, Quay-Peterson Behavior Problem Checklist, Behavior Rating Profile, Piers-Harris Self-Concept for Children, Burks' Behavior Rating Scales, Behavior Evaluation Scale-2, informal assessments, and observations.

☐ **OCCUPATIONAL THERAPY** (To be administered by a licensed occupational therapist)
Purpose: These tests assist in determining if services by an OT may be required to assist a child with a disability to benefit from special education. Tests may include, but are not limited to: Peabody Developmental Motor Scales, Test of Visual Motor Skills, Bruininks Oseretcky Test of Motor Proficiency, Test of Visual Motor Skills-Revised, informal assessments, and observations.

☐ **PHYSICAL THERAPY** (To be administered by a licensed physical therapist)
Purpose: These tests assist in determining if services by a PT may be required to assist a child with a disability to benefit from special education. Tests may include, but are not limited to: Battelle Developmental Inventory, Peabody Developmental Motor Scales, informal assessments, and observations.

☐ **OTHER**
Purpose: _____
_____

Continued Staffing Notes

☑ **Continued Staffing Notes**　　☐ **Updated Eligibility Information**　☐ **Discipline IEP**

☐ **Exiting Special Education - IEP Completed**

Name: Brandon　　　**Student #:**　　　**Date of Birth:**　　　**Date: 7-16-08**

Notes:

Brandon attended Extended School Year at Coralwood(6-09-08 to 7-17-08) . Brandon had perfect attendance for the summer. When Brandon arrive to school in the morning , he would greet you after you have greeted him first. Brandon made some progress using scissors and required hand over hand assistance. He was able to trace his name with assistance of the teacher. Brandon did an outstanding job using the toilet and did not have any accidents . We did have to remind him to was his hands on occasions and he did not indicate when he had to use the restroom. He went when the rest of the class was taken to the restroom.

Brandon's Spring score are as followed Brandon will cut out shapes with straight lines:2%,Brandon will print his first name:2%,Brandon will improve social skills in area of interaction with others:5%, Brandon will use the toilet :5%.

Brandon's Pre-Sm score are as followed Brandon will cut out shapes with straight lines:20%,Brandon will print his first name:10%,Brandon will improve social skills in area of interaction with others:20%, Brandon will use the toilet :80%.

Brandon's Post-Sm score are as followed Brandon will cut out shapes with straight lines:10%,Brandon will print his first name:15%,Brandon will improve social skills in area of interaction with others:25%, Brandon will use the toilet :90%.

There will be a meeting Brandon 2-3 weeks after school begins in August 08-09 by the classroom teacher to review ESY progress. Brandon's teacher will need to retest his ESY goals & objectives and record fall data.

APPENDIX D
DR. CHRIS GREENE (APPOINTMENTS)

Appendix D

Dr. Chris Greene (Appointments)

Patient Schedule

Basic + Hair Analysis

Brandon
12/7/2007
ation Date: Next week

INSTRUCTIONS

ed Hair Analysis

c. 14 @ 2:30

PRODUCT	Upon Waking	Breakfast	10:00 AM	Lunch	3:00 PM	Dinner	Before Sleep		
Malvin	5 drops – 3x day								
Dopamine	5 drops – 3x day								
Taurine	5 drops – 3x day								
Butter oil	½ TSP – 2x day								
Cod Liver – HIGH DHA	TSP – 2x day								

December 13, 2007

Christopher Greene, DC
1982 Highway 78
Main Street East #D
Snellville, GA 30078

Re: Brandon ̄

Dear Dr. Greene:

In reviewing Brandon ̄ ̄ ̄ ̄ ̄ ̄ ̄ ̄ recent tissue mineral analysis, mineral pattern deviations have been revealed which should be modified in order to achieve optimum biochemical balance.

Lead toxicity, in individuals of all ages, is a major source of ill health today; however the adverse effects caused by lead toxicity are greatly magnified in children. Numerous metabolic dysfunctions are linked to lead toxicity, inasmuch as lead in the body tissues affects the levels of every other mineral in the body. With this knowledge, Brandon's high lead level of 6.587, in conjunction with his low sodium/potassium ratio of 0.57/1, is of major concern. Research reveals that when toxic levels of lead co-exist with a sodium/potassium inversion, various symptoms are often present in children, such as learning disabilities, hyperactivity, behavior problems and emotional problems.

Inasmuch as the release of insulin is promoted by calcium and inhibited by magnesium, the proper ratio of calcium to magnesium is critical for optimal insulin secretion, thus resulting in one's ability to properly metabolize sugars and carbohydrates. In addition, the adrenal glands play a major role in regulating carbohydrate, fat and protein metabolism in the body. A low sodium/potassium ratio is indicative of excessive glucocorticoid production. Potassium reflects glucocorticoid levels (sugar hormones), while sodium reflects mineralocorticoid levels. When the mineralocorticoid hormones get out of balance with the glucocorticoid hormones, an individual will develop a sensitivity to the ingestion of sugars and simple carbohydrates.

Taking the above into consideration, Brandon's calcium/magnesium ratio of 13.00/1 and his low sodium/potassium ratio of 0.57/1 are indicative of a sensitivity to the ingestion of sugars and simple carbohydrates. Accordingly, it would be most wise for Brandon's parents to eliminate sugars and simple carbohydrates from his dietary intake at this time, including fruits and fruit juices, even the unsweetened kind. These are very high in glucose and other sugars and can have the same detrimental effects as candy and other sweets. (See enclosed list of foods). This will perhaps not be easy for them to comply with, however it will prove to be very rewarding in the long run. This recommendation is very important.

ARL ANALYTICAL RESEARCH LABS, INC.

Research indicates that it is not at all uncommon for tumors of all kinds to be associated with a sugar and simple carbohydrate sensitivity.

It is well known that lead displaces calcium from tissue storage reserves and as a consequence, Brandon's high lead level could be playing a contributing role for his sugar and carbohydrate sensitivity at this time inasmuch as such a displacement of calcium could contribute greatly to a deviant calcium/magnesium ratio.

Brandon's zinc level of 8.00 is low indicating a loss of zinc from the tissues, resulting in a zinc deficiency. A zinc deficiency, for whatever reason, is frequently associated with the impairment of normal insulin activity inasmuch as zinc is required for the production of insulin, release of insulin from the pancreas and for prolonging the action of insulin. This, in turn, is also a probable contributing cause for one's inability to metabolize sugars and simple carbohydrates.

Tissue breakdown (protein), or catabolism, is a common finding in individuals exhibiting a low sodium/potassium ratio. With the inability to properly digest and utilize foods consumed, the body begins to break down storage tissues in an effort to maintain homeostasis (a state of equilibrium of the metabolic process), and adequate energy levels. Body proteins are broken down into amino acids for conversion into sugars to produce energy in an attempt to maintain homeostasis. Enhancing Brandon's ability to properly metabolize sugars and simple carbohydrates should, by reducing protein catabolism, contribute positively to his health status. Such being the case, it would be advisable for Brandon's parents to increase his dietary protein intake by 15 percent.

It is important that Brandon's parents understand that his low sodium/potassium ratio and his high calcium/magnesium ratio are often associated with chronic stress, which may be due to nutritional deficiencies, toxic metal accumulation, or external stress. This combination of ratios is a common mineral pattern in children and may be accompanied by feelings of frustration at times. While the diet and supplement program may assist in eliminating the nutritional causes for stress, it may also be helpful if Brandon's parents would encourage him to express any concerns he may be having.

It is not at all uncommon for individuals, particularly children, with a severe sodium/potassium inversion to suffer from bed wetting problems, particularly if the individual is a fast oxidizer, which Brandon is.

Brandon has an iron level of 1.6. Although low hair iron may be associated with anemia, in many cases it is not. The hair iron may only indicate tissue iron reserves. Inasmuch as copper is necessary for the attachment of iron to the hemoglobin molecule, his low copper level of 1.00 (normal being 2.50) may be contributing to his low iron level at this time.

A consistent finding in autism is an extremely low tissue copper, or bio-unavailability of copper (less than 1.00 mg%) inasmuch as a bio-unavailability of copper in linked with severe disorders of the central nervous system. The books Biological Treatments for Autism and PDD by William Shaw, Ph.D. and Autism and Pervasive Developmental Disorder by Karyn Seroussi are an excellent source of current information on autism.

Brandon also has a presence of cadmium (0.021). Cadmium is an extremely toxic metal which has no known necessary function in the body. In addition, cadmium toxicity contributes to a large number of health conditions and deviant mineral patterns.

In addition, Brandon has a high level of the toxic metal aluminum (9.07). A high aluminum level is frequently caused by the taking of antacids for digestive distress. Another common cause of aluminum toxicity relates to the drinking of soda pop and/or other beverages from aluminum cans.

Young children, particularly under the age of six (6), normally cannot swallow whole supplement tablets. We recommend that the supplements be crushed and mixed with a small amount of strong flavored foods such as peanut butter, apple sauce, yogurt, tomato sauce, soup, etc. This method usually works very well. For crushing tablets, a new easy-to-use device called EZE-Crusher is available from Endo-met Labs for your convenience.

Brandon's adherence to the recommended supplement program, together with following the dietary recommendations will be helpful in obtaining optimal biochemical balance.

The information in this letter is for educational purposes only. If you have any questions regarding Brandon's tissue mineral analysis, please do not hesitate to contact our office.

ANALYTICAL RESEARCH LABS

ARL ANALYTICAL RESEARCH LABS, INC.

2225 W. Alice Ave. • Phoenix, AZ 85021 USA • (602) 995-1580

Christopher Greene, DC

PATIENT NAME:	Brandon				
SEX: M	AGE: 5	DATE: 12/13/07	LAB NO. 411963	CLIENT ACCT. NO.	95008

NUTRIENT MINERALS

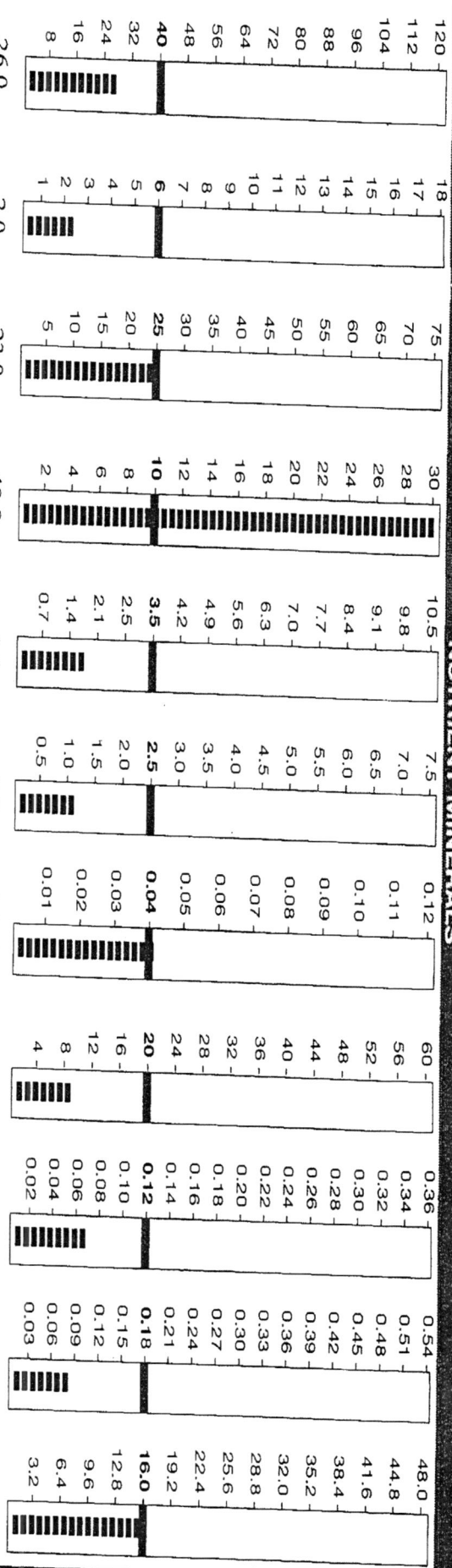

Element	Previous Test
CALCIUM (Ca)	26.0
MAGNESIUM (Mg)	2.0
SODIUM (Na)	23.0
POTASSIUM (K)	40.0
IRON (Fe)	1.6
COPPER (Cu)	1.0
MANGANESE (Mn)	0.041
ZINC (Zn)	8.0
CHROMIUM (Cr)	0.062
SELENIUM (Se)	0.075
PHOSPHORUS (P)	15.0

TOXIC METALS

Element	Previous Test
LEAD (Pb)	6.587
MERCURY (Hg)	0.011
CADMIUM (Cd)	0.021
ARSENIC (As)	0.006
ALUMINUM (Al)	9.07

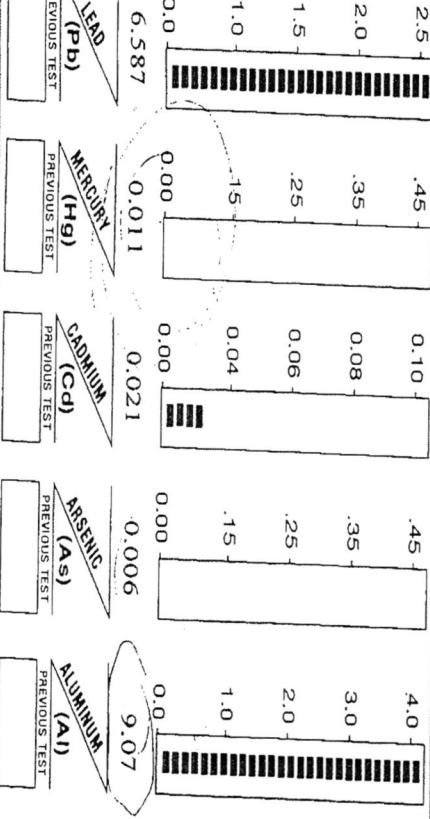

ADDITIONAL MINERALS

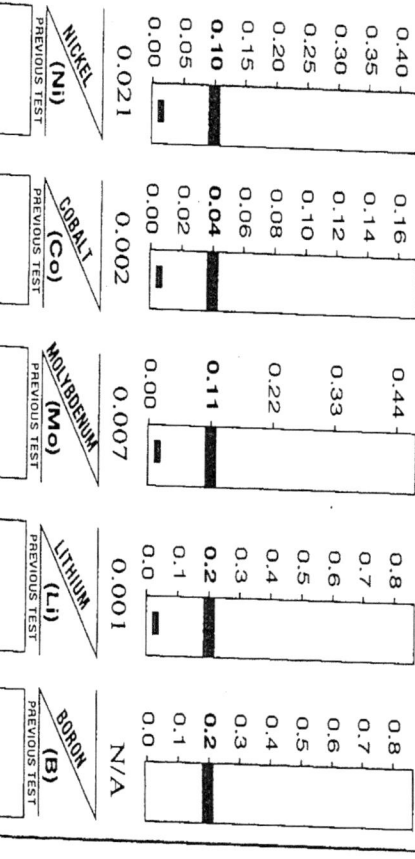

Element	Previous Test
NICKEL (Ni)	0.021
COBALT (Co)	0.002
MOLYBDENUM (Mo)	0.007
LITHIUM (Li)	0.001
BORON (B)	N/A

SIGNIFICANT MINERAL RATIOS

MINERAL RATIO	IDEAL RATIO	CURRENT RATIO	% OF IDEAL	PREVIOUS RATIO
CA/MG	6.67	13.00	195	
CA/K	4.00	0.65	16	
NA/MG	4.17	11.50	226	
NA/K	2.50	0.57	237	

LOW — IDEAL — HIGH

panvers
sugar
Myaird
Adrenal

Patient Schedule

Follow-Up

Patient: Brandon
Date: 12/14/2007
Re-evaluation Date: 3 weeks

SPECIAL INSTRUCTIONS

- Follow-Diet

NO Gluten / Past. Milk
Lower Sugar

PRODUCT	Upon Waking	Breakfast	10:00 AM	Lunch	3:00 PM	Dinner	Before Sleep		
BIOKUIT									
Week 1		1				1			
Week 2		2				2			
Week 3		3				3			
Week 4-11		3				3			
Week 12-15		2				2			
Maintenance		1				1			
Acetylaldehyde 5 drops - 3x day									
All else same									

Patient Schedule

Follow-up

Brandon
2/8/2008
Date: 4 weeks

STRUCTIONS

PRODUCT	Upon Waking	Breakfast	10:00 AM	Lunch	3:00 PM	Dinner	Before Sleep		
Flush-eez		2 squirts 3x day							
resume Blofult									
Adrenal Support		8 drops - 3x day							
METOX		5 drops - 3x day							
Camu Powder		½ TSP - 3x day							
~~Chlorella 4tp~~									
All else same									

Standard Process.

Patient: Brandon

Date: 3/20/2008

Re-evaluation Date: Re-Scan graf 3

SPECIAL INSTRUCTIONS

Blocked - Left ear
chemicals

April 29 @ 5:00pm
Dr Dan

Patient Schedule

Follow-up

PRODUCT	Upon Waking	Breakfast	10:00 AM	Lunch	3:00 PM	Dinner	B S
ChemiTox		8 drops - 3x day					
HealthBac		1 teaspoon/day					
E3 8		6 drops 2x day in water					

Nutri-Energetics Infoceutical Protocol

Name: Brandon   Date: 4/29/2008

N|C

- Take Infoceuticals in the order listed below starting with "1"
- Take infoceuticals separately. Do not mix unless directed to do so.
- Place indicated number of drops in a glass of spring water and drink immediately
- Leave at least 10 minutes between taking each infoceutical

Info	Day	1	2	3	4	5	6	7	8	9	10	11	12	13	14	15	16	17	18	19	20	21	22	23	24	25	26	27	28	29	30	3
1	PL	6	6	6	6	6	9	9	9	9	9	15	15	15	15	15	28															
2	ED6					6		6				6	6	6	6	9	9	9	9	15	15	15	15	28								
3	ED10				6			6				6	6	6	6	9	9	9	9	15	15	15	15	28								
4	ED13					6			6	6	6	6	6	9	9	9	9	15	15	15	15	28										
5	ESSA	9 or 15 or 28 drops 2-3 x day										9	9	9	9	15	15	15	15	28											
6																																
other																																

During the first 7-10 days when starting on infoceuticals, you may have a detox reaction (this is not a side effect as there are not biochemical substances in these products). Detox means that the body is attempting to eliminate toxins. You may notice changes in color or smell in urine, bowel movements, minor irritability, sores or bumps under the skin or in mouth or tiredness. Stronger detox reactions include nausea, headaches and interrupted sleep. If this happens, stop taking preparations for 3 days then resume taking them at dosage reduced by 50%. If you have questions, please call. These energetic preparations will not interfere with supplements, prescription drugs or herbal preparations.

Recommendations:

_____

_____

_____

Next appointment Date:_____ Time:_____

Nutri-Energetics Infoceutical Protocol

Name: **Brandon**   Date: 6/13/2008

2 VISIT

- Take Infoceuticals in the order listed below starting with "1"
- Take infoceuticals separately. Do not mix unless directed to do so.
- Place Indicated number of drops In a glass of spring water and drink immediately
- Leave at least 10 minutes between taking each infoceutical

Info	Day	1	2	3	4	5	6	7	8	9	10	11	12	13	14	15	16	17	18	19	20	21	22	23	24	25	26	27	28	29
1	ED9	6	6	6	6	6	6	6	6	9	9	9	9	9	9	9	15													
2	EI8			6	6	6	6	6	6	6	9	9	9	9	9	9	15	15	15	15	15	28								
3	EJ10			6	6	6	6	6	6	6	9	9	9	9	9	9	15	15	15	15	15	28								
4	ES8		same as last TIME																											
5	ESR		6 drops 3x day → 9 drops → 15 drops																											
6																														
other		2 minerals																												

During the first 7-10 days when starting on infoceuticals, you may have a detox reaction (this is not a side effect as there are not biochemical substances in these products). [ ] means that the body is attempting to eliminate toxins. You may notice changes in color or smell in urine, bowel movements, minor irritability, sores or bumps under the skin o[ ] the mouth or tiredness. Stronger detox reactions include nausea, headaches and interrupted sleep. If this happens, stop taking preparations for 3 days then resume taking th[ ] a dosage reduced by 50%. If you have questions, please call. These energetic preparations will not interfere with supplements, prescription drugs or herbal preparations.

Recommendations: #4 & 5 Stay on

Next VISIT ETO

ET8

Next appointment Date: 4 weeks   Time: Wed. July 16 4:45

Nutri-Energetics Infoceutical Protocol

Name: _Brandon_   Date: _7/16/2008_

Follow UP 1/2

- Take Infoceuticals in the order listed below starting with "1"
- Take Infoceuticals separately. Do not mix unless directed to do so.
- Place indicated number of drops in a glass of spring water and drink immediately
- Leave at least 10 minutes between taking each Infoceutical

Info	Day	1	2	3	4	5	6	7	8	9	10	11	12	13	14	15	16	17	18	19	20	21	22	23	24	25	26	27	28	29	30	31
1	ED3	3	3	3	3	3	6	6	6	6	6	9	9	9	15	15	15	15	15	15	28											
2	ED8	6	6	6	6	6	9	9	9	9	9	15	15	15	15	15	28															
3	EI7	6	6	6	6	6	9	9	9	9	9	15	15	15	15	15	28															
4	ET4 (9)	6	6	6	6	6	6	6	6	6	9																					
5	ES5 (15)	6	6	6	6	6	6	6	6	6	9	9	9	9	9	9	15	15														
6	ES8																															
Other	ESR / Same																															

During the first 7-10 days when starting on infoceuticals, you may have a detox reaction (this is not a side effect as there are not biochemical substances in these products). Detox means that the body is attempting to eliminate toxins. You may notice changes in color or smell in urine, bowel movements, minor irritability, sores or bumps under the skin or in mouth or tiredness. Stronger detox reactions include nausea, headaches and interrupted sleep. If this happens, stop taking preparations for 3 days then resume taking them at dosage reduced by 50%. If you have questions, please call. These energetic preparations will not interfere with supplements, prescription drugs or herbal preparations.

Recommendations: _1st Time To Speak Since Beginning. Gave name / Birthday_

Next appointment Date: _30 days_   Time: _Aug 20 @ 11:00_

Nutri-Energetics Infoceutical Protocol

Name: Brandon   Date: 8/28/2008

Follow up

- Take Infoceuticals in the order listed below starting with "1"
- Take infoceuticals separately. Do not mix unless directed to do so.
- Place indicated number of drops in a glass of spring water and drink immediately
- Leave at least 10 minutes between taking each infoceutical

Info	Day	1	2	3	4	5	6	7	8	9	10	11	12	13	14	15	16	17	18	19	20	21	22	23	24	25	26	27	28
1	ED4	6	6	6	6	6	9	9	9	9	9	15	15	15	15	15	28												
2	ED6	6	6	6	6	6	9	9	9	9	9	15	15	15	15	15	28												
3	EI9	6	6	6	6	6	9	9	9	9	9	15	15	15	15	15	28												
4	ET7	6			6			6	6	6	6	6	9	9	9	9													
5	ES10	6	6	6	6	6	9	9	9	9	9	15	15	15	15	15	28												
6	ES8	same																											
other	ESR																												

During the first 7-10 days when starting on infoceuticals, you may have a detox reaction (this is not a side effect as there are not biochemical substances in these products) means that the body is attempting to eliminate toxins. You may notice changes in color or smell in urine, bowel movements, minor irritability, sores or bumps under the sk the mouth or tiredness. Stronger detox reactions include nausea, headaches and interrupted sleep. If this happens, stop taking preparations for 3 days then resume takin a dosage reduced by 50%. If you have questions, please call. These energetic preparations will not interfere with supplements, prescription drugs or herbal preparations.

Recommendations:

Cod liver & Butter oil
1TBSP   1TBSP

Next appointment Date: 2 & 4 week   Time: SEPT 16 @ 5:00
Oct ? @ 5:30

APPENDIX E

09/02/2008 WRITTEN TRANSCRIPT OF DR. CHRIS GREENE'S
"WAKE UP TO NUTRITION" RADIO SHOW
(FEATURING LYNNE GEORGE AND LAURIE LEDBETTER)

"WAKE UP TO NUTRITION" RADIO SHOW
WITH
DR. CHRIS GREENE

September 2, 2008

Guest Speakers: Lynne George *and* Laurie Ledbetter

[*Music interlude*]

WGUN presents the most comprehensive and cutting-edge health show on radio today—*To Your Health with Dr. Chris Greene.* And now, here's your host, Dr. Chris Greene.

[*Music interlude continues*]

DR. CHRIS: Hi, welcome back everybody to another segment of to your health. I'm your host Dr. Chris Greene. I'm glad to have you with us. We have a power-pack show today that I am excited to get to rolling. And, this—our beginning of our fifth year of being here at WGUN. It's hard to believe that four years—August 30th, 2004—that we started our show here. And, going into our fifth year now, we have been trying to bring you as much education that we can squeeze into one hour every day for the last four years. Today is no exception. Normally I, you know, I talk about education and being able to enlighten people in relationship to what's going on with themselves, their families, their bodies and how we're being affected environmentally and how we're being infected about the choices we make on a day-to-day basis. This is no exception today. As now, I'm bringing in the grandmother of one of my patients to tell her story in relationship to her grandson. We'll get to her in just a moment. But, I want you to understand some things that I think is very important. Earlier this year, we had on CNN, and I normally don't like CNN—and I'll just tell you up front—but typically, I'd just go there for brief news bits—albeit bias news bits on—from Fox News of being bias to CNN being bias, but anyway, you look at it from this perspective. Byron Richards, who I respect a lot, who is a certified clinical nutritionist had written a great article on CNN helping to uncover the autism debacle that was blowing up in our government's face, and what we were talking about was on April 2nd, they spent a day bringing awareness of the problem of autism. They had Larry King's segment which included at the time Jenny McCarthy and Jim Carrey talking about her son who is autistic and her role of being able to bring him back from autism. And, make no mistake that it can be done. Here's the problem that I have is when people come in, as a practitioner, what you want is a patient that is actually going to follow the advice that you give them, and many people come in with the expectation that there's going to be in one or two visits, that their life is going to be turned around. You have to understand that a lot of the situations that we have today, and we're going to be talking about autism, in particular, but it doesn't really matter whether it's autism, whether it's Alzheimer's, whether it's any type of neurodegenerative disease, any type of autoimmune disease. All of these things have a common thread that you have to look at and really understand that it's going to take time to peel back layers that have been existing for a number of years. Now, when we look at—I'm going give you a brief history, and then we're going to get to our guest today—of what's going on—when we look at the history of the vaccinations, the profits and the motivations of politics that go behind this, then we have to understand the what the big pharmaceutical companies are doing and realizing that vaccines have been used for over a hundred years. Germ warfare is part of that, and so what we look at, they really engrain in us that that vaccinations is a part of our National Security, and it's in our National Security interest for everyone to be vaccinated, and so— part of the problem that you see with like military personnel is that they're really the pin-cushions, initially, the experimented that are experimented upon, to be able to go through and have all of these vaccinated people as they go overseas or whatever. When we look at that, and I'm going to read a couple of things from a couple of different people. First, there's going to be Byron Richards and his take on this. Then, we're going to go to Dr. Philip Incao who's going to describe the immune system and how this works. And, we're going to get into Lynne George who is a patient of mine's grandmother. And, we're going to talk about the changes that we've seen in Brandon, her grandson, and his return from autism. So, you don't want to miss this, because if we have to take it into two parts, we will, and we'll bring in tomorrow with our good friend Stuart as we talk about the brain and inflammation, and what we have to do to quell that information. I like this with Byron. It goes that... *[t]he government knows full well that there will be deaths and injuries from vaccinations, collateral damage that is justified by a prevented disease, a convenient and fear-driven, fear-mongering risk factor here or tactic.* He goes... *[i]magine having a calculator that always has the same conclusion no matter what data is entered into it.* I like that. It's almost like an *Alice In Wonderland* approach. No matter what you put into the calculator, it comes up with the same answer. So, he asks... *how can the risk of injuring 1 in 150 children.* And, I think that risk is now is even worse than that—*for life.* For life. Do you understand that 20 years ago that injuring—it was 1 in 10,000 kids that had autism—1 in 10,000. Now, we're at 1 in 150. Part of this folks is the idea—see, what's happening is, is that you have so many people that are saying that it is because of the Thiomersal, and because they're removing the Thiomersal—which is the Mercury—from the vaccines, they're mandating—well, you see, it's really not the Thiomersal or it now, you see, it really wasn't because we removed it. You see, well, it's not just that, and we're going to talk about what that is; okay. He goes, *[h]ere's the thing: 1 in 150, how can that be acceptable? Any business,* as he would say here... *would love to have the opportunity to produce a product and have the government mandate its sale*—in other words, forced us to be able to go in and take this vaccination; you see. And, he says... *government officials find lucrative jobs in the industries that they regulate after doing "good work." Autism is partly a side-effect of the cancer within the government agencies. Our government will never pay the price to screen children at risk for autism.* Why? It's too much money, too proactive, too expensive on the front end. Where does the cost lie in treating an autistic children—in our autistic children? With the family, you see. The families have to foot the burden, and make no mistake, it's hard—it's difficult, because I know an autistic child is very difficult to handle, you see. And so, he goes... *[t]he problem for our government is that an admission of guilt on the autism vaccine link causes the entire paradigm of the big pharma-driven, western-medicine sickness industry to collapse. Even worse in their eyes, it would send an earthquake through the brotherhood of big pharma, public health, the CDC, the FDA, the global elite, and the military. Other public health problems—programs would be in question, like polluting our water with a neurotoxin called Fluoride that makes a population more docile and controllable,* you see. The problem is, and I agree with him—he goes... *[u]nfortunately, for parents combating autism, the problem for their child is only a portion of the issue they must now try to solve.* They're up against the government dead set on preventing the truth on ever coming out, based on the damage that's being done. And, what we refer to is the case here, in Atlanta, of Hanna Poling who is nine years old now who finally admitted—it was finally admitted—and this was the first case of 4900 autism cases that were pending. Basically, she claimed that the Mercury containing vaccines were the cause of her autism, and that the Federal Government, at that point, conceded that this autism case, saying that it is compensation that is appropriate. So, it is an admission of guilt at this point, but again, they were saying, well, the CDC is saying that it was a mitochondrial disorder, because remember that the mitochondria are the little powerhouses of the cell that help drive cellular respiration and create the energy. We'll talk more about that in just a moment, but he says... *[o]ur government is using various studies to deflect the vaccine-autism link*; okay. See, again, according to Byron, it says, however, neither Thiomersal nor any single vaccine is an adequate overall explanation for autism. And, I would have a tendency to agree. What is it then that's creating the problem? You understand that over the last 20 years, we've gone from children five or six vaccines—me growing up and remembering some of those—to now where a child before the age three or four is getting up to 48 shots, and it's the collection of these adjuvants—okay, the collection of these adjuvants that are creating the problem here; okay. That's what creating the problem, and so, the—you know, as we look at the MMR and like the Thiomersal activity problem—obviously, there's going to be a link there, because what we're looking at is creating an inflammatory cascade—that's what these adjuvants do—to illicit an immune response, you see. That's what's going on, but now, let's look that some of the adjuvants that are in there, and I'm just going to mention a few here: aluminum hydroxide; aluminum phosphate; aluminum potassium sulfate; various amino acids; ammonium sulfate; brilliant green, which is a dye; you have things that I can't even pronounce, okay; fetawing (sp?), which is a bovine serum protein; formaldehyde, which is a carcinogen; formalin; gelatin; gentamicin; glycerin; human serum albumin—we've done shows *ad nauseum* on some of these adjuvants and their carcinogenic causes that they create in the body. You have so many polys in here. I can't name them all. You have various antibiotics. You have sugar. You have obviously Mercury. You have yeast proteins that are creating problems here. This is why, and I want to read this specifically about how your brain works and how these—and I want you to have an understanding of what we had to do with Brandon and being able to reduce and quell this inflammation; okay. What we have is the current government strategy is to keep arguing about Mercury and the MMR vaccines, because they will create enough doubt and say, well, it's not the vaccines that's creating the problem, but I want you to—I want to read this, and I want you to understand what's going on and how the brain works. The vaccines contained weakened signatures of a disease that by themselves are not strong enough for the immune system to mount a response. This problem is solved by adding a booster compound called an adjuvant, which I just went over and gave you some of the things that are in these vaccines. And see, here's the problem. It's that most people are going to their doctors and not asking what is in this vaccine. By the way, just wanted to—just for your own edification and understanding in here, did you know that a lot of these vaccines have aborted fetal cell line products? The chicken pox virus, for instance, Avero vax has aborted fetal cells. So does that Hepatitis A virus—or vaccine—so does the Hepatitis B; the MMR; the Polio; the Polio combination which has the DTP; the Polio; the HIB and the Hep B, together. Can you imagine giving your child all of that at one time? The Rheumatoid arthritis vaccine; the Sepsis vaccine; the Shingles vaccine; the new Small Pox vaccine all have aborted fetal cells; okay. Did you know that? Did you want that injected into your body? It's bypassing the body's natural response mechanism here. He goes... *[i]t is cleric.* Let's read this... *[A]n adjuvant does not contain any signature of the disease; rather, the adjuvant initiates an inflammatory reaction which is the first step in any immune response. The idea is to get the immune system revved up*—remember that as we go through this—*so that it can see the weakened disease and learn what it looks like so that if it ever sees it again, it* will be more prepared to fight it. *This concept, in and of itself, has validity but only given the right set of circumstances.* He goes on... *[i]t is clear that those with autism have an excessively inflamed brain.* I will also say an excessively inflamed gut—so that we have the gut and the brain connection. *If pressed, the CVC would likely argue that the brain inflammation is result of the autism and that they need more studies to determine the cause.* And I like what Byron says. He goes... *I will argue that they don't need any more studies at all and that the cause is blatantly obvious based on an understanding of existing science—the multiple inflammatory insults from the adjuvant and vaccines at a rate of 1 in 150 cases sets the brain on fire and causes the autism directly. As in a side and to a lesser extent, but just as important to society, a minor brush fire causes ADD, ADHD—an impaired intelligence.* So, if your child does not suffer from autism, he does suffer from impaired intelligence. So, let's quickly go through briefly how the brain works, and I'm going to give you this. I'm going to read you this verbatim, because I don't want to miss anything, because I want you to understand. He goes... *[t]he crumbling paradigm of western medicine likes to break down body function according to convenient classifications, such as nerves immunity and hormones, etc.* Now I—I want to think about that. Are we just a bundle of nerves? Well, sometimes, I am. But, are we just an immune system? No. Are we just hormones? No. We are collectively all of those things working in concert, like a fine-tuned symphony, if we're running appropriately. He goes... *[i]n reality, your brain is a central processor* like Intel. I'm hoping that we don't cut ourselves open and find Intel stamped on us, but anyway, *a central processor of all systems in your body and thus has connections that link nerves, immune function and hormones into one symphony of functions.* In other words, it is not possible to study only neurotransmitters like serotonin or dopamine and actually understand what your brain is doing. You see, if we just take that—that's like isolating a particular vitamin and saying *that is the vitamin* and forgetting all of the other components that go with that. Do you understand that this is why we can't study just one pesticide to see what implication it's going to have on the inside of our body, because there's more than just one that we're being exposed to. It's a conglomeration or synergistic compilation of all of these things together. He goes... *[t]en percent of the cells in your brain are neurotransmitter related*—ten percent. *The other 90 percent are glial cells called astrocytes. For decades, scientists thought that the 90 percent of your brain was nothing more than a structural framework, simply because scientific tools were not adequate to understand what the glial cells were doing.* Just because we don't understand something doesn't mean it's not happening. Just want to reiterate that; okay. *But that has changed in the past ten years because glial cells now run you brain and your neurotransmitters. They are the powerbrokers, if you will, of all the information coming into you brain which directly links to your immune system and your endocrine system creating the hormones. Glial cells are the inflammation brokers in your brain.* So, when we have stress, remember—when I went through and we talked about adrenals, what we were talking about was that there were four major types of stress—we had the chemical, the physical, the emotional—all these things going on. How did your body respond to stress? In the exact same way. It didn't matter whether it was an emotional component or a traumatic event or you were physically harmed or whether you had a tremendous amount of chemical toxicity. Your body responds to the exact same, it perceives that stress the exact same way. So, when we have stress, a toxin that's polluting our bodies, destructive food additives like MSG, aspartame, food colorings, when they enter your brain, they induce what we call the excitotoxin reaction. This is from Russell Blaylock's work. *Excitotoxins: The Taste That Kills*—the book. He goes... *[t]hey inflame brain cells. This inflammation is now buffered primarily by a hormone called leptin and other antioxidants*; okay, but this is what—that process is what keeps your glial cells healthy, but when these buffering mechanisms—these anti-inflammatory capacity of your glial cells is overloaded or overburdened, let's say with—let's say a child getting seven different vaccinations with at least 40 or 50 adjuvants. Then, what's happening is, is that you have an overload that creates more wear and tear than the brain can handle. When minimally—this results in brain wear and tear, but he goes on to say... *[i]t is the mechanism behind all accelerated brain aging.* So, is that what we're doing when we're overloading a child's nervous system that is not even fully developed—an immune system that is not fully developed—are we not overloading that and accelerating brain aging and depending on a person's genetic weakness and other health issues, leads to these various states of cognitive decline and nerve-related diseases of aging, such as Alzheimer's. There is also a point in which low-grade brain inflammation catches fire. In adults, we see that this is, let's say, related to Parkinson's or the spreading of depression, you see, because it causes a power outage in our head. He goes... *[s]uch an event is typically triggered by emotional pain or physical pain of a prolonged nature or acute intensity which leads to elevated substance "P" levels— normally high—abnormally high levels, and this pushes your nerves over the edge.* The difference in a fetus or a small child—okay, remember that you can pass on fat-soluble toxins—which we'll talk about here—to your developing fetus; okay—your baby that is developing inside. The difference in a small child is that the nervous system is still rapidly evolving. If the brain catches fire at this age, then the proper development of the nerves are seriously disturbed, which is the full autism spectrum of disorders—like Asperger's and on—so on—or like ADD, ADHD or a lower IQ level in a child. He goes... *[t]he adjuvants in vaccine is pro-inflammatory. In other words, neurologically excitotoxic. This is intentional so as to boost the effectiveness of the vaccine. The problem comes about when given so many of them at once which can even a perfectly healthy child. Giving multiple adjuvants is like playing Russian-Roulette with a child's brain. Children with already inflamed nerves are at a much higher risk for reacting to multiple vaccines as their nerves have been conditioned to hyper-react.* So don't think that the folks at the CDC don't know this already. Alright, I'm going to give you a few examples of things that can cross over into the blood brain barrier; okay, but environmental pollution; fat-soluble toxins. Alright, things that are in our food supply like pesticides, which remember, that many of the pesticides that we are being exposed to were originally used in the Natzi concentration camps as nerve agents; okay, but here's another thing on children, especially, mothers that are not nursing. Iron fortification of baby formulas—this encourages the growth of hostile bacteria and candida albicans in the digestive tract. Now, you add on top of that an antibiotic, and then, because of ear infection, and then you give your child a vaccination with all of the adjuvants. Do you not think we're setting up a recipe for disaster and autoimmunity problems and allergy problems, which we will discuss here? If we don't get to it today, it will be on tomorrow's show. Also, C-Section deliveries also increase the risk for these hostile bacteria and candida to grow and malfunction; okay. With that, I'm going to introduce my guest—I've given you a long dissertation into understanding of what happens in the brain, and we're going to be talking more about it here in just a moment. Alright. And why these vaccines are so—I tell you, it's just amazing what we're seeing with this, and you have to do your homework. With that, I'm introducing the grandmother of one my patients, Brandon, and her name is Lynne George, and I'll tell you, if we could all have a grandmother that was like this, that took an active role in this autistic child's case, we would all be fine. And, with that, I'm going to introduce Lynne George. Lynne, you're going to have to talk right into the microphone. How are you this morning? Thanks for joining us this morning here.

LYNNE GEORGE: And, thank you for having me, Dr. Chris.

DR. CHRIS: Lynne, go on and get a little closer to the mike. There you go. Very good. And, so Lynne, give us a brief overview of why you're here today.

LYNNE GEORGE: The reason why I'm here today is to discuss with people and, you know, to let them know how wonderful—first of all—God is, and how He's opened this window of opportunity. And, Brandon's autism—reversing it—is a culmination of everything. First of all: God and prayers; and you, Dr. Chris—the way you—first of all, the things that you did—his hair analysis. The first time he went for a visit, you didn't do anything. You made sure that you got into it to where you knew exactly what was going on with him. So, can you tell us about the hair analysis?

DR. CHRIS: One of the things that we look at—obviously, we've talked about hair analysis on this. One of the things that we have to look at is that many times we're measuring stress in the body, and people think most of the time, I'm just looking for minerals; right? I'm looking for heavy metals. That's an important component. There's no doubt. The other component though, is that we're looking at the endocrine system and how it's being stressed. We're looking at how the body is metabolizing sugars, the stress on the adrenal—as we talked with the hormones, the thyroid, the pancreas, protein utilization so that we know that the body is in a catabolic—tearing down phase, or is it in an anabolic phase, which is rebuilding? Many times, especially with the spectrum of autism disorders that we're looking at, we're seeing that most of these children are in a catabolic state. In other words, their tissues are breaking down faster than they are repairing, and this was the case with Brandon, and what we saw is that his body was breaking down so much quicker than it was able to repair. And, that he had—he did, in fact, have heavy metal toxicity. So, we approached it from that standpoint. Now Brandon is how old now?

LYNNE GEORGE: Brandon is five years and nine months.

DR. CHRIS: Five years and nine months. So, our first official visit after the hair analysis was in March. So, that was when he was about five years and four months.

LYNNE GEORGE: Four months [said in unison with Dr. Chris].

DR. CHRIS: Yes. And so, tell us what Brandon—I mean, so Brandon, here he was at five years and four months. Tell us the problems that you were having with Brandon at that time.

LYNNE GEORGE: Okay, at five years and four months, this is something that I've gathered— that I've also received his diagnosis and evaluations from when he was a year and got into Early Steps. Brandon could not communicate. He was non-verbal. He could not process to understand. He also has a brother whose 15 months older, and he did not play with him nor any other child—so, he isolated himself. He couldn't gesture. He flapped his arms like he was about to take off in flight. He had temper tantrums, and he cried for everything, everywhere we brought him. I mean, it was just constantly.

DR. CHRIS: I remember.

LYNNE GEORGE: Okay. He banged his head on soft objects, especially when he was sleepy. He did a lot of stimming—stimming, which is opening his mouth and shaking his hands. Hitting his head. He would spin himself. He would spin objects. He didn't like change. He cried uncontrollably. Even though cried all the time, it was uncontrollably when he couldn't communicate.

DR. CHRIS: See folks, just as we talk about autism as a statistic, the problem is, there's a face with those stats, and there's—see there's a lot of heartache and torment with those. It's not, Lynne? I mean, this is the family trying to hold it together to be able to take care of someone. See, it's already stressful enough of living this life.

LYNNE GEORGE: Exactly. It takes a toll on everyone.

DR. CHRIS: And so, now we look at when you're having someone that you're having to take care of that is typically uncontrollable.

LYNNE GEORGE: Right, and it's 24/7, except when he's asleep.

DR. CHRIS: Right.

LYNNE GEORGE: And, even though when he's asleep, because we have to check on him all the time.

DR. CHRIS: Sure, sure—go ahead. Continue.

LYNNE GEORGE: Okay. His eating habits. That was really the strong point, because his habits—the doctor was telling us, as long as he's eating, and all he craved was like oatmeal cream pies, chocolate milk, *Cheetos*, bread—but—

DR. CHRIS: He was—

LYNNE GEORGE: You know, he just didn't want to eat—

DR. CHRIS: —craving those, but there were reasons for that.

LYNNE GEORGE: Right. And then, we still had to force him to take a bit of things, so he wasn't eating properly, and then he was really out of the box, like you know, super hyperactive.

DR. CHRIS: Right. Right. Well so, I mean, when we look at this, I mean he didn't laugh. There was no potty training, because he wore Pull-ups. He had no social skills. He had no eye contact. I mean, there was a lot of things that we see here. We don't have to cover all of them today, but needless to say, there's at least 30 items that you have here that he could not do—

LYNNE GEORGE: Right.

DR. CHRIS: —at five years and four months.

LYNNE GEORGE: Exactly.

DR. CHRIS: Now, what I want you to go through—then, we're going to about what we did with Brandon in a minute. Now, here it is, he's five years and nine months, what are the major changes that you've seen since we've put him on the program?

LYNNE GEORGE: The major changes that we've seen are so numerous, and like—

DR. CHRIS: It's almost something like he's changing every day.

LYNNE GEORGE: Right. It's like Christmas every day. Okay, Brandon says his name. You can ask him a question yourself, and I know you were excited, because—

DR. CHRIS: I was.

LYNNE GEORGE: —he said his name and his date of birth.

DR. CHRIS: Right.

LYNNE GEORGE: But, the tripping part was is when he walked out of the office, and he read your sign.

DR. CHRIS: He's reading.

LYNNE GEORGE: "Caution: Wet paint on all doors."

DR. CHRIS: Now, the thing that, I guess, blew me away on that is that most kids can't even read at that age, but here's a child—now, before he came in, there was no communication.

LYNNE GEORGE: None whatsoever.

DR. CHRIS: No verbal communication whatsoever—hardly any eye-contact. Now what we're seeing is that he is reading.

LYNNE GEORGE: He's reading. He reads books. He can read anything and everything. He can even spell over 300 words.

DR. CHRIS: And now we're seeing that—he was in the office last week, and that's what prompted me to bring him on today is because, folks he is—it is like Christmas. He's coming out of his shell, and we're seeing visual contact—he's making eye contact with me. He's able to sit in the chair and do the testing that we do on him.

LYNNE GEORGE: Exactly.

DR. CHRIS: And, but he—I mean, what I liked, Lynne, is the approach that you took—is that you took boxes of words, and he's learned to spell these words. He's learned to make sentences and talk in complete sentences.

LYNNE GEORGE: It's like he was in—he was there, but he just couldn't get out. So, I went and I got these blocks that he had, and he was able to express himself. The blocks are—had four letters on each block, and there's 48 blocks, and he started spelling small words. So, May 31st was my birthday.

DR. CHRIS: Right.

LYNNE GEORGE: And, he was on a table, and he was sitting down and he started spelling. He spelled over 100 words just that day, and it was just amazing.

DR. CHRIS: I mean, to me, because when he first came in, there was just the—in March, it was like to be able try to test him—we couldn't actually test him.

LYNNE GEORGE: Exactly.

DR. CHRIS: We had start with some basic things, because we did not—he did not want to—you know, he was crying; he was afraid of me; afraid—and there was no eye contact. Now, he's looking at me in the eyes. He's giving me a high-five before he walks out of the office. He's reading anything that we want him to read. I mean, for him to read that sign, it did floor me. I've got to be honest with him.

LYNNE GEORGE: He even read your Labor Day sign. Closed—

DR. CHRIS: Right.

LYNNE GEORGE: —that you were closed.

DR. CHRIS: —on Labor Day. [LAUGHTER] Right.

LYNNE GEORGE: Yeah.

DR. CHRIS: So, what are some of the other social skills that you're seeing with him?

LYNNE GEORGE: Social skills? Let's see. He can catch a ball. He's plays with his brother now, and his brother always wondered why my brother is not playing—

DR. CHRIS: —playing.

LYNNE GEORGE: —with me. So, he's playing with his brother. He loves going to Chuckie Cheese, and he's getting on every little ride at Chuckie Cheese.

DR. CHRIS: Right.

LYNNE GEORGE: He was even on the horse, and we were all so elated, and before, we couldn't get him in the door, because he cried going into a social place.

DR. CHRIS: And, of course, we're not eating stuff at Chuckie Cheese.

LYNNE GEORGE: No.

DR. CHRIS: Just want to let you know that. [LAUGHTER]

LYNNE GEORGE: Exactly. We'll get to the diet part later of—

DR. CHRIS: Absolutely. Right.

LYNNE GEORGE: —what we're giving.

DR. CHRIS: But, I'm looking at here—he's learned to catch a ball—to throw a ball. And, he's doing flash cards. He's giving hugs now. Right?

LYNNE GEORGE: And, you can feel the love with hug.

DR. CHRIS: So, it's almost like thank goodness I can actually feel. He's emotion now.

LYNNE GEORGE: Exactly.

DR. CHRIS: And, he's being able to—he's able to express that emotion.

LYNNE GEORGE: Uhm hum.

DR. CHRIS: Whereas before, it was like, he just couldn't do that.

LYNNE GEORGE: Yes. The first—what happened was, the eighth day that we were going through the nutrients and the homeopathic—what happened with Brandon was is lymph nodes were swollen.

DR. CHRIS: Right. Exactly.

LYNNE GEORGE: Okay, this was eight days, and we were kind of scared, and we—

DR. CHRIS: Right.

LYNNE GEORGE: And you were so wonderful, because we could you 24/7 to find out what was going with him, and you said, just be patient. He's going to go through this, and he's going to come out of it. Well, let me tell you about when he was being detoxified. He had to go to the bathroom a lot. So, that's the purging of all of these uh—

DR. CHRIS: Toxins.

LYNNE GEORGE: Toxin out of his body.

DR. CHRIS: Now, Lynne, I gave a dissertation on the brain and some of these adjuvants in the vaccinations.

LYNNE GEORGE: Uhm hum.

DR. CHRIS: Brandon received a full onslaught of vaccinations.

LYNNE GEORGE: He sure did.

DR. CHRIS: And so, I'm not saying that that's what's causing it, but we know that there's a lot of inflammation there.

LYNNE GEORGE: Well, we know that he was normal—

DR. CHRIS: Right.

LYNNE GEORGE: —because everything was going on point.

DR. CHRIS: Right.

LYNNE GEORGE: —until right after the vaccinations, he just shut down completely.

DR. CHRIS: Right.

LYNNE GEORGE: He just was like a zombie.

DR. CHRIS: Right.

LYNNE GEORGE: He was there, but he wasn't.

DR. CHRIS: And you told me before we went on the air, and I did not realize that he had received one set of vaccinations where it was seven different vaccinations in one shot.

LYNNE GEORGE: Yes. You know, it was seven different shots in one day. [See Brandon's immunization record for exact number of shots administered.]

DR. CHRIS: That's right. That's right.

LYNNE GEORGE: Yes.

DR. CHRIS: In one day. That's correct. So, from that standpoint, it's almost like you saw the light in his eyes go—

LYNNE GEORGE: Yes, it was—all of a sudden, he just shut down completely. He didn't talk. He didn't—he was just there—

DR. CHRIS: Right.

LYNNE GEORGE: —just a body there. He would just look out the window all the time, and we noticed it, but then when other people—visitors, relatives—

DR. CHRIS: They're going—

LYNNE GEORGE: —they're going like what's wrong with him?

DR. CHRIS: Right.

LYNNE GEORGE: That's when, you know, we saw the picture, and then he was walking on his tippy-toes.

DR. CHRIS: Right.

LYNNE GEORGE: And, he would see objects like a fan—a ceiling fans—he would start waving and getting excited, and could see almost his heart jumping out of his chest, because you could see it moving—

DR. CHRIS: Right.

LYNNE GEORGE: But, nothing was coming out. Nothing.

DR. CHRIS: So, he couldn't express himself. So, now what we have is a situation. As you went through the detox, you did see changes in bowel structure. I mean, you know his habits there, and we were pulling a lot of stuff out; weren't we?

LYNNE GEORGE: Well, the first eight days were really rough, because he had a lot of diarrhea. It was liquid.

DR. CHRIS: Right.

LYNNE GEORGE: And, he didn't eat. He was lethargic, so he slept for light four days, and afterwards, he started—I guess his throat was hurting a little bit, but he started sipping the nutrients and eating the bananas, and we were still giving him the nutrients, but, you know, he rested a lot, but by the eighth day, he had the rash on him.

DR. CHRIS: Right.

LYNNE GEORGE: And, we called you—

DR. CHRIS: Right.

LYNNE GEORGE: —and you were just guiding us through everything, and rash disappeared in one day, and then his skin just glowed, and I noticed something, because I was there by myself, and I was walking in the other room, and somebody said, "what are you doing Nanna?", and I turned around, and were the only ones in the house, and it's like, "what did you say?" So, he said that, and then, later on that day, he was doing something mischievous, and he said, "oh-oh!"

DR. CHRIS: So, he was recognizing everything—

LYNNE GEORGE: Yes.

DR. CHRIS: —that going on. So see, folks, part of the situation is that he went through a detox, which many of us, I know, sometimes are afraid of, but guess what? Living in this world, because we don't live in a bubble, we are exposed to these things, and it was just the natural consequence of what we were seeing that we knew that we had to get this out him to be able to have the inflammation quell, so to speak, for him to be able to recover.

LYNNE GEORGE: Exactly.

DR. CHRIS: Uhm, he is basically now on computer games. He's doing like the Leap Frogs; right?

LYNNE GEORGE: He's doing everything. First of all, he's doing Leap Frog, he's spelling words. He's constantly learning. He's like a sponge who wants to learn.

DR. CHRIS: It's like he—like all of it—

LYNNE GEORGE: Yes. He's hungry.

DR. CHRIS: He's hungry for this knowledge.

LYNNE GEORGE: Uhm hum.

DR. CHRIS: So, in other words, his brain now is able to develop.

LYNNE GEORGE: It's developing. Yes.

DR. CHRIS: So, there were some things that were blocking that. Let's—let's talk about this, because I want to give Laurie Ledbetter in here with us—here in just a moment, but let's talk about some of the things that we did with Brandon and what brought about this transformation. So, let's go through, first of all, first thing that we said from day one, we had to change his diet; didn't we.

LYNNE GEORGE: Change his diet completely.

DR. CHRIS: So, no more oatmeal cream pies.

LYNNE GEORGE: No. No more of that, and he doesn't even want it. That's what's so wonderful.

DR. CHRIS: And so, one of the things that we did, folks, is change his diet, and of course, I mentioned the book, and Tony, let's go ahead and bring on Laurie Ledbetter who is a rep for Natasha McBride. Laurie, good morning. How are you this morning?

LAURIE LEDBETTER: Good morning, Dr. Chris, I'm doing wonderful.

DR. CHRIS: Good. Listen, Laurie, you're hearing this story about this transformation about this little boy Brandon at five years of age, and it's just kind of like, you know, this is, Laurie—this is the reason I got into what I'm doing right now.

LAURIE LEDBETTER: Yes.

DR. CHRIS: I mean, this is to me what warms your heart, because you're hopefully making an impact in someone that has been altered, really not by choice.

LAURIE LEDBETTER: Yes.

DR. CHRIS: And so, the way I look at it here is that part of the staging I'm going to give, you know—I've a multiple of things here. This is just one of it, but one of things that we had to look at is Natasha McBride's work, and we've talked about her book on this show before, "The Gut and Psychology Syndrome," and the importance of controlling or quelling, if you will, the inflammation of autism here.

LAURIE LEDBETTER: Yes.

DR. CHRIS: Let's go into that about what this diet really is entailing.

LAURIE LEDBETTER: Well, it—what Natasha's looking at—first of all, I wanted to say that listening to that story is just breaking my heart, and I hear similar stories that are happening across the United States. And, a lot of this is due to the great work that you're doing and also the discoveries that Natasha Campbell-McBride discovered, and what she discovered through her clinic in the UK as well as working with her son who is autistic, was there was this inflammation that you talked about, and there was a correlation between the inflammation in the blood and the inflammation in the brain and how important it was to start seeing the kind of results that you're seeing is to stop this inflammation, to work with the diet, eliminate the foods that she has listed in her book that would allow the gut to heal, and then also introducing a probiotic—the one that she uses is Bio-Kult, which I think—

DR. CHRIS: That's exactly what Brandon used.

LAURIE LEDBETTER: —Brandon used. And, it is a therapeutic probiotic that you introduce at a very slow rate into the diet so that when you start building up this bacteria, and it starts doing what's supposed to do that the [INAUDIBLE] does not occur, you know, too fast and slowly, because then all of a sudden, you start having this bacteria in your gut—this healthy bacteria that is acting as an antifungal, antibacterial, antiviral, anti-panacea, and it starts bringing balance to your immune system and getting it working again.

DR. CHRIS: And this is really—Lynne, this is really what we've seen with Brandon. I mean we talk about the detoxification. We used the Bio-Kult. We used the diet. Folks, I think—if you have a child that is suffering from autism, if you do not follow this diet, I think you're going to be spinning your wheels, because you have to reduce the inflammation in the gut. We had to reintroduce—now what made the Bio-Kult unique, Laurie, in relationship to Brandon's case?

LAURIE LEDBETTER: Uhm. I think what was unique to his case is that, well you have to back up a little bit to notice that one of the things that Natasha says that why our children are in this situation and to begin with is that many moms are giving birth today that grew up on what we call the sterilized food supply that we have, sort of engrossed ourselves into—

DR. CHRIS: Sure.

LAURIE LEDBETTER: —in the United States' culture, and you talk about all the time about what in a western foods and whole foods, but we all grew up on these foods—this fast food supply, and what it has done to the women in this country is that it has affected their immune system which is their gut, so they aren't getting these raw food or natural foods. Everything is pasteurized or sterilized from your juices to your honey to your dairy products to everything.

DR. CHRIS: See, that is affecting our whole immune system.

LAURIE LEDBETTER: Exactly.

DR. CHRIS: Now, I'm going to try to go through this quickly. I may repeat it on tomorrow's show. I want people to understand about the immune system and how this works. This is actually from Dr. Philip Incao, and he has described the immune system thusly. This is going about a page, but I want to go through it and read it, because I think it's very, very critical. He goes... *[i]t is composed of two functional branches or compartments, and they work together in a mutually, cooperative way or in a mutually antagonistic way, depending on the health of the individual. One branch is what we call the humeral immune system, which is TH2, for short, and this is producing the antibodies in the blood circulation as a sensing or recognizing function of the immune system to the presence of foreign antigens. In other words, we have foreign proteins, but we also have proteins to our tissues that have been damaged. That creates these natural tissue antibodies. So the humeral phase of the immune system is what produces antibodies to these foreign proteins and proteins to self; okay. The other branch is the cellular or cell mediated immune system; okay—which again destroys, digests and expels foreign antigens out of the body through cells that are produced through the thymus, your tonsils, your adenoids, your spleen, and your lymph nodes and lymphatic system.* Lynne, this is what we were seeing that was being really worked on through Brandon; was it not?

LYNNE GEORGE: Exactly.

DR. CHRIS: See, here's what's happening. You're going to understand why Brandon had the result that he did. In other words, his lymphatic system started to get congested; right?

LYNNE GEORGE: Right.

DR. CHRIS: You'll understand that here in just a second. He goes... *[t]hese two functional branches immune system may be compared to the functions in eating—tasting and recognizing the food on the one hand and digesting the food and eliminating the food waste on the other.* So the humeral phase, which is the antibody phase, is the taste and recognizes and even remembers foreign antigens for years and years and years. This is why I like people—I don't know if you saw this Laurie, but the people that had the 1918 Spanish flu—

LAURIE LEDBETTER: Yes.

DR. CHRIS: —90 years later are still producing antibodies to that flu. Ninety years later; okay.

LAURIE LEDBETTER: Wow.

DR. CHRIS: Now, the cellular phase of the immune system is what digests and eliminates these foreign antigens from the body; right? But, he goes... *[j]ust as too much repeated tasting of food will ruin the appetite, so also too much repeated stimulation of the tasting humeral immune system by an antigen will inhibit and suppress the digesting and eliminating function—in other words, the cellular function—which is*—where is that coming from? That's what... *[c]reating organisms*—excuse me—*the white blood cells from your thymus, your tonsils, your adenoids, your spleen, your lymph nodes.* You see, that process, by the way, of destroying and digesting and discharging these foreign antigens is a normal, acute inflammatory response, but guess what it's accompanied by? Inflammation, fever, pain, malaise—this is what exactly went through; isn't it?

LYNNE GEORGE: Brandon had fever and everything.

DR. CHRIS: See, that had been suppressed in him.

LYNNE GEORGE: Uhm hum.

DR. CHRIS: Now, you're going to understand why in just a minute. He goes... *[t]his explains the polar opposite relationship between acute discharging inflammations, on the one hand, and allergies and autoimmune inflammations on the other*—which is what we're seeing with people that are over-vaccinated are these sky-rocketing tendencies to allergies, asthma and autoimmune conditions. He goes... *[t]he more a person has of one, the less he or she will have of the other. A growing number of scientists believe that the increase in America, Europe, Australia, and Japan in allergic and autoimmune diseases which stimulate the humeral response, which is*—remember, that's your antibody response; okay—*is caused by the lack of stimulation of the cellular response of the immune system from the lack of acute inflammatory responses and discharges in childhood.* We've become too germaphobic. He goes... *[w]e need to identify the factors which cause this shift in the function of the immune system or which cause allergies and autoimmune diseases in childhood to increase.* He goes... *[n]ow, they're going back to the vaccination.* Now let's look at this. He goes... *[i]f we now return to the original question of the mechanism of adjuvant vaccinations; we find that what, I believe, is the key to the puzzle of vaccinations consists of introducing a disease agent.* Remember, that's what I talked about in the beginning of the show—*or disease antigen into an individual's body without causing the disease. If the disease agent provoked the whole immune system into action, it would cause all the pain of the disease, which is primarily the symptoms of fever, pain, malaise, loss of* *function of the acute inflammatory response of the disease.* So, the trick of a vaccination is to stimulate the immune system just enough so that it makes antibodies and the remembers the disease antigen but not so much that it provokes an acute inflammatory response by the cellular immune system and makes us sick with the disease that we're trying to prevent. Thus, a vaccine works by stimulating very much the antibody production; okay, and by stimulating very little or not at all of the digesting and discharging function of the cellular immune system. So vaccine antigens are designed to be unprovocative or indigestible for the cellular immune system, thereby weakening it.

LAURIE LEDBETTER: Uhm hum.

DR. CHRIS: Now, what we did with Brandon is that we brought a lot of this crap that had been put into his body and that his body had compensated for, we started bring it to the surface.

LAURIE LEDBETTER: Moving it out.

DR. CHRIS: Moving it out. He goes... *[p]erhaps, it is not difficult to see then why the repeated use of vaccines would tend to shift to the functional imbalance of the immune system toward the antibody producing side and away from the acute inflammatory discharging side.* He goes... *[t]his has been confirmed by the Gulf War Veterans. Most vaccinations cause a shift of the immune function from the TH1 side, which is the cell the mediated side to the TH2 side, which is creating chronic autoimmune or allergic responses.* So, what we look at—he goes... *[w]hat in reality is prevented is not the disease but the ability of our cellular immune system to manifest, to respond and to overcome the disease. "There is no system of the human being from mind to the muscles, to the immune system which gets stronger through avoiding challenges but only through overcoming these challenges.* You see, this is why we've seen the difference with Brandon in that regard is that we actually are no getting his cell mediated immunity springing back into action. Does that make sense, Laurie?

LAURIE LEDBETTER: Yes, absolute. And, that's what the probiotics, the therapeutic use of probiotics and healing the gut actually does.

DR. CHRIS: Well now, I'm going to go ahead and mention, because I want to get Lynne back in here. Lynne, the other things that we've done with Brandon, we've put him on cod liver oil. We've done some Camu Camu. We did the Flush-EZ, but more importantly, we did also with the Bio-Kult, the diet, which you guys have followed to a "T", but you did note that when he sneaks things, you can see a reversion—a reverting back to old ways; don't you?

LYNNE GEORGE: Yes, like if he would sneak a piece of bread or something like that, you can notice the reversion, because he doesn't pay attention. He's not as directive. He can't—

DR. CHRIS: Right.

LYNNE GEORGE: —you know—he's just out of control a little bit, but then, once he gets his nutrients back in him, he's fine. He can—it takes a couple of hours if he sneaks something, and so, once he's on this healthy regime, he has to stick with it the rest of his life.

DR. CHRIS: He will. Go ahead.

LAURIE LEDBETTER: And one thing that Natasha has found though is that if you follow the program that she discussed in her book is increasing these probiotics, you know, every week—

DR. CHRIS: Sure.

LAURIE LEDBETTER: —for up to eight weeks, sometimes particularly autistic children, it can take up to two years. So, she does say that you can get you can get to a point where the gut can be healed to the point where you do not have to follow Brandon around. It takes time like you said, Dr. Chris. This is not going to be healed over night. You cannot do it. It's not going to absorb in a couple of months. It is going to take time to repair the damage, but she has found not only with her patients but with her own son that she does not have to following around anymore, that she can go on vacation, and as he eats some of these foods that would normally cause this horrible reaction, that he can eat it and it does not cause the reaction, then they go back home and get back on the diet. So, there is a sort of some hope in there from what she see is that it can be healed to a very large degree, not that you can go back to the old way of healing and eating that caused this situation in the beginning, but that you can venture into that world of eating every once in a while and come out of it and not see the reactions that you see. So, I would say just hang in there and keep working with those probiotics, because it just takes a while to heal the gut.

DR. CHRIS: Laurie, I found that—and this is something that is real critical hear, I'm really astounded that how quickly Brandon has come along.

LAURIE LEDBETTER: Yes. Yes.

DR. CHRIS: That I thought it was going to take longer.

LAURIE LEDBETTER: Yes.

DR. CHRIS: And then the thing is what's disheartening, I guess, is sometimes that you get the parents of these children and they don't give it the time.

LAURIE LEDBETTER: Yes. You've got it the time, Dr. Chris. And you have to give it the time. It—it took a lot to get to this situation, and it takes take to heal, and if you're patient with it and work it like you said, and also, the younger you begin the process, the faster the healing occurs, and you'll just start seeing results like you've seen with Brandon.

DR. CHRIS: Lynne, you brought out a great point. If we had been following this from the time that you first noticed it, how much further would Brandon be? I guess that was really your question; wasn't it?

LYNNE GEORGE: Yes, because I'm amazed that, you know, it's only been going on the fifth month. You know, like I say, he doing something new every time, but I was asking you if we would have started it like when we noticed it like after 17 months, when he was diagnosed and evaluated—

DR. CHRIS: Right.

LYNNE GEORGE: —with autism, you know, what kind of—

DR. CHRIS: Results would you have seen.

LYNNE GEORGE: —yes, results.

DR. CHRIS: The other thing that I think that you were frustrated about is the lack of people doing this and recognizing that these problems in the first place.

LYNNE GEORGE: Yes.

DR. CHRIS: I mean, was that not one of the key factors here that there was an—

LYNNE GEORGE: Yes.

DR. CHRIS: —area of frustration?

LYNNE GEORGE: I was frustrated, because, you know, attorneys are going to seek restitution. That's fine. You know, and doctors are going to try find a cure, but what's going on now with the person who has autism now. We have to have to help them now. You know, so I just looked at it and said, I have to help my grandson some kind of way, and I feel God has made me in a situation where I have a back debilitation, and I'm there all the time—

DR. CHRIS: Right.

LYNNE GEORGE: —to be with him, and they have to have that. They have to have—everything is a culmination of everything.

DR. CHRIS: You were talking about—because I was looking at this. You had kind of written this out, and I was going *Pizza and Lemonade*, but that's not the traditional pizza—

LYNNE GEORGE: Exactly.

DR. CHRIS: —that most people are thinking about.

LYNNE GEORGE: And, that's not the traditional lemonade.

DR. CHRIS: Briefly just go into what's in Brandon's pizza.

LYNNE GEORGE: Okay, what's in Brandon's pizza. Let's see, first of all, we use almonds, and I want to say uhm I've never talked you on the phone, but Natasha Campbell-McBride's book *Gut and Psychology Syndrome*, that is our reference book, that is like our bible to Brandon's autism, because we've read it back and forward and know exactly what the problem is—what the source is. So, to understand the source, that's how we can help him with his problem. But, in Brandon's pizza, we use almonds, because you can't use any type of—

DR. CHRIS: Of gluten—

LYNNE GEORGE: —gluten or anything.

DR. CHRIS: —at all.

LYNNE GEORGE: Yes, and they say gluten-free, casein-free diet.

DR. CHRIS: You can't even use that.

LYNNE GEORGE: You can't even have that.

DR. CHRIS: Right.

LYNNE GEORGE: So, it's almonds, and we use any type of meat—breast of chicken, mostly shrimp, but it's in sea salt and natural stuff. You can't season it with any type of seasoning, because that usually has sugar. Bell peppers, organic cheese, cloves of garlic, handful of baby spring mix, 12 natural slices of bell peppers, and he has this—every five days, we bake a pizza, and he has at least three slices a day. So, everything is natural.

DR. CHRIS: So, I mean, when we look at this, Brandon, and this is—folks, this is Brandon is recovering, because he's got someone at home that has taken the time, that's giving him his nutrients. The other thing that we've done with Brandon, of course, is that the Infoceutical scan—the NES scan. Laurie, you're familiar with that as well.

LAURIE LEDBETTER: I am.

DR. CHRIS: And, I think that the Energetic work that Peter Fraser and Harry have put together with that. I think it has been a culminating factor on why Brandon—

LAURIE LEDBETTER: Yes.

DR. CHRIS: —has recovered. The Energetic work in removing—the whole idea behind a NES scan is to remove the blocks—

LAURIE LEDBETTER: Yes.

DR. CHRIS: —that are impeding his healing. We also had Brandon on the Flush-EZ which was helping that bowel to open up and dump those toxins that had been stored in the liver—the gallbladder—

LAURIE LEDBETTER: Yes. And, Dr. Chris, I would say that I think that Energetic work is what's also allowing the body it heal itself as quickly as it can with these probiotics.

DR. CHRIS: I don't think it would have been as fast.

LAURIE LEDBETTER: No, I don't think so either.

LYNNE GEORGE: He was constipated up until five years, four months.

DR. CHRIS: Right.

LYNNE GEORGE: So, five years and four months, he was constipated.

DR. CHRIS: He was holding on to those toxins.

LAURIE LEDBETTER: Yes.

DR. CHRIS: Tony, do we have Corey on line with us yet. Go ahead and see if you can pull Corey up for me; all right, and—because I want to make sure that Corey gets on this morning, but, you know, as I look at this, Laurie, I guess to me it's just really kind of humbling and at the same time exciting to see a child return from the brink of non-communication here.

LAURIE LEDBETTER: Yes. It is overwhelming to see, but the great thing is that it's working, and it's simple, and we can do it with our diet. We can do it with the help of you and looking to make sure all of the other elements are in place, and, you know, it's bringing all these pieces of the puzzle together from all of these great people like yourself is what's making this happen—

LYNNE GEORGE: Exactly.

LAURIE LEDBETTER: And, we need to get the word out to as many people as possible, because what's important here, Dr. Chris, is we have 1 in 97 boys—

DR. CHRIS: One in 97?

LAURIE LEDBETTER: —that have autism in this country.

DR. CHRIS: Yes.

LAURIE LEDBETTER: This is our—this is our future, and if we don't address this with also reaching mothers who are about—mothers-to-be and letting them know how important it is to reestablish this bacteria, because when the child comes into this world, it has a sterile gut, and it gets that immune system and that bacteria by going through the birth canal and by breastfeeding. Then we have a generation of children that have not had that entrance way into this world.

DR. CHRIS: And, it's making them weaker as a result.

LAURIE LEDBETTER: Naturally. And, generation after generation, they're getting weaker. The first generation may be getting allergies and asthma. The second generation has the ADD, ADHD. And, the third generation is moving up into the autism spectrum, and so we need to look at that.

DR. CHRIS: All right. Real quick. I want to remind you, and this is, Lynne, you said in here, and I— when we started this program, initially Brandon's breath, for the first time smelled like weak-old garbage.

LYNNE GEORGE: Oh my goodness. It was horrible.

DR. CHRIS: And so, when he was congested, the lymph nodes in his neck were swollen. He could not swallow. He moved as though was neck was stiff.

LYNNE GEORGE: He couldn't breathe.

DR. CHRIS: So, I mean folks, this happens because these things are poisons in your body. So, he was tired. He slept. His body was recovering. This is what's going on. We've only got a couple of minutes. Let's go ahead and move to Corey with today's specials. Good morning Corey, how are you?

COREY: Doing great. How is it going?

DR. CHRIS: Corey, I think a very moving and touching show on what's going to me, and it's very enlightening to start our fifth year here.

COREY: Oh yeah, and if people want copies. We have copies available for people to re-listen. What we're going to be doing today is that some of the Bio-Kult probiotics and the book, along with that—you can get the Bio-Kult probiotic for $59.95 and the book for $29.95. In fact, you can get them together and take off an additional 10 bucks off of their normal price. You can get the two of them for $79.95, but the Bio-Kult probiotic that we have been talking about and the book, "Gut and Psychology Syndrome." We're also doing a couple of other things that relate to immune and bowel health, because they are so interrelated, especially when we're talking about probiotics. We've got the Cat's Claw formula by Whole World Botanicals, which is the Peruvian Cat's Claw which normalizes bowel health—helps with overall inflammation in the bowels and helps regulate intestinal—

DR. CHRIS: It also regulates inflammation throughout the body. That's—

COREY: Right.

DR. CHRIS: —one of our favorites. Go ahead.

COREY: Exactly. The Cat's Claw, we're doing at $19.95. That's normally almost a $30 product. It comes in a liquid. You can actually get three bottles of that today for $49.95. So you don't want to miss out on that. That's the lowest I've ever done that at.

DR. CHRIS: Corey. We've only got about a minute. Let me have you run through those pretty quickly.

COREY: Uhm hum, and then we've also got the Smooth Food 2 and the Probiotic Immune Support by New Chapter which also—the Smooth Food 2 helps with elimination, breathing on a daily basis to keep the bowels moving and the Probiotic Immune Support is a Probiotic formula from New Chapter that focuses on overall immune health as well. Most of those are 40% off of retail. All of these are available at Wake to

Nutrition. The number to call is 770-979-5825. Again, 770-979-5825. Toll free: 1-877-7AWAKE, and also check us out at WUTN.com.

DR. CHRIS: Also, the book—folks, we may be out of it, because I know Laurie—Laurie, you were out of the book.

LAURIE LEDBETTER: I am completely sold out, but I'll have them in two days.

DR. CHRIS: Yes. So, we'll have that order—and those orders filled. Probably, it will take us two to three days to be able to do that. So, be patient, but I think it is well worth it. Laurie, I appreciate you being with us. Corey, thank you for being for being with us. And, Lynne, we're going to try to bring you back tomorrow.

LYNNE GEORGE: Okay.

DR. CHRIS: And, just—I love the story. I love what's going on here. And, thanks for being with us as well today.

LYNNE GEORGE: Thank you.

DR. CHRIS: And, folks, any problems or questions in relationship with getting this, we'll have copies of the show. You need to give it to your friends. To me, getting the word out and understanding why we're seeing these spectrum disorders as we are, I think it is very, very critical. The number at Dr. Chris' Natural Pharmacy for appointments with myself and my associate Dr. Dan Fowler, 770-979-5125. That's 770-979-5125. Listen, you guys have a great day. We'll continue this discussion tomorrow with our good friend Stuart Tomkin. You guys take care. We'll talk to you then.

[Music interlude... Black Magic Woman]

RADIO STATION ANNOUNCER: YOU'VE BEEN LISTENING TO "TO YOUR HEALTH" WITH DR. CHRIS GREEN. JOIN US MONDAY THROUGH FRIDAY AT THE SAME TIME FOR ANOTHER NEW AND EXCITING SHOW. THE OPINIONS EXPRESSED ON THIS SHOW DO NOT NECESSARILY REFLECT THOSE OF THIS STATION AND SHOULD NOT REPLACE THE ADVICE OF YOUR PHYSICIAN. IF THERE ARE ANY CONCERNS ABOUT DRUG INTERACTIONS, PLEASE CONTACT YOUR QUALIFIED HEALTH CARE PRACTITIONER.

[THE END]

APPENDIX F

09/03/2008 WRITTEN TRANSCRIPT OF DR. CHRIS GREENE'S "WAKE UP TO NUTRITION" RADIO SHOW (FEATURING LYNNE GEORGE AND STUART TOMC)

"WAKE UP TO NUTRITION" RADIO SHOW
WITH
DR. CHRIS GREENE

September 3, 2008

Guest Speakers: *Lynne George and Stuart Tomc*

[*Music interlude*]

WGUN presents the most comprehensive and cutting-edge health show on radio today—*To Your Health with Dr. Chris Greene.* And now, here's your host, Dr. Chris Greene.

[*Music interlude continues*]

DR. CHRIS: Alright. Welcome back everybody to another segment of to your health. I'm your host Dr. Chris Greene. Thanks for spending an hour of your time with us each and every day here Monday through Friday at WGUN Radio. You can listen also live to us at the internet at www.wgunradio.com, and as always, it's Wednesday. It's my good friend and colleague, Stuart Tomc[i] that's going to be joining us this morning. I want to remind you also that you can call Dr. Chris' Natural Pharmacy. The number there is 770-979-5125. That's for appointments with myself and my good friend Dr. Dan Falor[ii] who is there. One of us is usually there Monday through Saturday for appointments. I'll be there through Saturday this week. I hope you guys are doing well. We had a very good talk yesterday with our good friend and Lynne George and Laurie Ledbetter.[iii] And, we were talking about Brandon, her grandson, his recovery or how he's really—we're seeing the reversing of autism with him, and we're going to talk a little bit about this morning. We've also got some things that we need to do with Stuart about some new studies on fish oil that has come out about heart failure. And I also want to talk about this issue with cholesterol and how low cholesterol actually increases cancer and death risks. This is a shot that's being heard quite prevalent now, and so, can we get cholesterol levels too low? Absolutely. What is cholesterol? It's a repair substance. That's what we have to remember. With that, let's go ahead and go to our good friend, Tony—Stuart Tomc—this morning. Good morning. How are you this morning?

STUART TOMC: Hey, Doc, I've never had a bad day in my life.

DR. CHRIS: Stuart, I didn't think you did, but I just thought I'd ask. I uh [LAUGHTER]. So Stuart, where are you calling from this morning?

STUART TOMC: *Chicago... that's* [SINGING]

DR. CHRIS: Yes. That is my kind of town. And, Stuart, how are you? I mean, really, how's things going?

STUART TOMC: It's fantastic. I just escaped from Hurricane Gustav.

DR. CHRIS: Right. You were down in New Orleans last week; were you not?

STUART TOMC: We were starting—we started in Shreveport, and we drove down right to the eye of the storm. And, I have a quick story I wanted to share with you. I did not know that in Shreveport, Louisiana, they have some internationally acclaimed school for the blind.

DR. CHRIS: Okay. I did not know that either; but go ahead.

STUART TOMC: People from all over that lose their vision—I know last time that we were talking about macular degeneration.

DR. CHRIS: Yes.

STUART TOMC: People that lose there vision come down there as adults—and listen to this a confident-builder—confidence builder. They teach you how to make furniture… blind.

DR. CHRIS: Wow.

STUART TOMC: So, I met a man that just went through the program. He heard about my talk wanted to come learn more about fish oil for macular degeneration.

DR. CHRIS: So, they don't call them stumpy anymore; right?

STUART TOMC: Can you believe this?

DR. CHRIS: [LAUGHTER]

STUART TOMC: [LAUGHTER] Imagine. You have to make a cabinet with dove-tail joints.

DR. CHRIS: Oh my gosh.

STUART TOMC: I mean, I've got 20/20 vision, and I can't do that right?

DR. CHRIS: Yeah, I can't do that either. Anyway, yeah.

STUART TOMC: Band saws and blades. No special protective gear.

DR. CHRIS: Wow.

STUART TOMC: Which is amazing to me, and so, it was a great trip. So, I got to meet those folks and go to—you know, talk to people that went through school. And, we just started going south, and I got out right in the nick of time—right before Gustav hit.

DR. CHRIS: Well, and uh—you know I understand. What is the full scale of that? Do we have any indication yet?

STUART TOMC: Well, looks like it was a beautiful miss for New Orleans. I'll tell you, the folks that I was with down there—the sales rep—he was born and raised down there. I'm paranoid, and he said, "No-no-no. Relax. Relax. We're going to do the dinner trainees. We're doing the trainees." He waited until the last second to get—in case this thing went east or west.

DR. CHRIS: Right.

STUART TOMC: And, that's what you get for, you know, he's a local. You know, he knew to wait. So, he went east. He went your way, while the storm went west. So, it was really, really great to meet those folks. Now, this was interesting. Just I noticed in your neck of the woods, people throughout the entire state down there, they were very hungry for cutting-edge information. So, I want people to know, especially down in that part of the country, you've some of the most hungry people for the truth and for the knowledge—anywhere that I've seen in the country.

DR. CHRIS: Stuart, I think that's really what we're seeing. People are tired of a lot of the rhetoric. At least a lot of the people that I've talked to. They're tired of the rhetoric and really getting nowhere with the same-old, same-old. So, we're trying to prevent—present to you a lot of new and cutting-edge information that is really, I think, is just that—cutting edge, and Stuart, yesterday, we had on the show Lynne George whose grandson is a patient of mine—Brandon. And, we—it was a very interested show, because what we're seeing is Brandon is taking steps to reverse the steps of autism, and we're seeing some real dramatic changes within from communication to being able to really be calm and learn and read and write, and we're going to bring Lynne on now. Tony, let's go ahead and get Lynne on and have her join this conversation. I know, Stuart, you have a lot of information that you can share with us that you and I talked about this morning about autism and some of the things that we've seen with fish oil and things like that, but, Lynne, good morning. How are you this morning?

LYNNE GEORGE: Good morning everybody.

DR. CHRIS: Glad to have you back with us, Lynne. Yesterday, we talked about, you know, really the odyssey that you're going through, and you have actually been filming this odyssey. So, we'll have something that we'll have a visual picture of this Stuart that we can actually see and the changes that are going with Brandon.

LYNNE GEORGE: Yes. That's correct. There's so many changes that I had to start documenting, because it was just numerous. And, let me tell you my Christmas present that we received yesterday. Little Ant came home, and he was so excited. Brandon and Anthony go to the same school. That's Brandon's older brother by 15 months, and he said when Brandon sees him, and he goes, "Hi." And, he waves to him. So, he was so elated. That was the first thing he told me when he came through the door.

DR. CHRIS: Well again, Stuart, Brandon ended up really falling into autism about the age of 17 months. I started working with him at about the age of five years, four months, and just briefly, again Lynne, Brandon had really not really communicated his whole life until recently.

LYNNE GEORGE: Until exactly four—almost five months ago.

DR. CHRIS: Right.

LYNNE GEORGE: And it was just an onset. It just kept going. Everyday, it was something new. And it was like sometimes two or three new different things a day. So, it's really exciting.

DR. CHRIS: What are some of the things Lynne that you know we didn't get to yesterday that you wanted to kind of share with our listening audience about what you're seeing with Brandon.

LYNNE GEORGE: Okay. He knows his name. He knows how to spell his full name. And, Thibodaux is not an easy name to spell for a last name.

DR. CHRIS: No it is not.

LYNNE GEORGE: He knows his date of birth. He says his age. He knows everybody's name. He has three grandmothers. He has Grandmommie; I'm Nana; and he has Grandmother. He knows his father's name; his brother's name. He knows Philippians 4:13. He can recite that Psalm [verse]. He knows how to state his night prayers. He can sing Donnie McClurkin, "We Fall Down and [but] We Get Up." The Pledge of Allegiance. He can dress himself—all the way up to his shoes, and if he has Velcro shoes, he can do that also. He cleans up behind himself, and he loves playing these educational games like V-Smile and V-Tech—things like that. He—by being potty-trained, meaning that he goes to the bathroom on his own. Now, we leave the door open for him so we can see him to make sure that he is washing his hands and, you know, doing things like that, but he does everything on his own. Number 1 and number 2.

STUART TOMC: How old is he?

LYNNE GEORGE: He is five years and nine months now.

STUART TOMC: Beautiful.

DR. CHRIS: To me, the other thing that you've noticed—you know—his immune system seems to be improving.

LYNNE GEORGE: He has not been since March, and we've been sick. Everybody has had some sort of virus or cold or something. Brandon has not been sick one day. Thank you, Jesus.

DR. CHRIS: And I guess, when I saw Brandon last week, he knew the months of the year, and then he was also—we were asking him mathematic equations, and he was able to respond to those.

LYNNE GEORGE: Yes. He knows 1+1, 2+2, 3+3, 4+4, 5+5. And he under—the thing is, he just doesn't say it. He knows. Like the words that he knows—the two to three hundred words that he knows, he can you tell you the vocabulary. When I was in Florida with my parents, he wrote the word "hiccup." And we go Brandon, what is that? And he goes, you know [MAKES THE HICCUP SOUND].

[CHUCKLE]

LYNNE GEORGE: And he made the sound. So, everything, he's writing—not writing but spelling the words. He can tell you what it means. That's what so phenomenal.

DR. CHRIS: This is not just rote memorization. What we're seeing is actually understanding of—

LYNNE GEORGE: And processing it.

DR. CHRIS: Processing.

LYNNE GEORGE: Uhm hum.

DR. CHRIS: That's to me, Stuart, the critical thinking skills that we're—that we're starting to re-establish with him that I think is so exciting here.

STUART TOMC: Did you also, doctor—did you put this young man on a gluten-free diet as well?

DR. CHRIS: Oh absolutely, we did. It was critical. In fact, Natasha McBride who wrote the book about "Gut and Psychology Syndrome," that was kind of like a preface, because obviously, the gut is like the second brain, if you will, using a lot of the neurotransmitters. We talked about inflammation in the brain with the glial cells and communication between the cells in the brain and how the gut plays a critical role in that, and then we talked about how that when we we're over-vaccinating people, it's setting the state for chronic autoimmune conditions, tissue destruction, as well as, going through and creating chronic states of allergy and inflammation that sets of asthma and those type of childhood illnesses.

STUART TOMC: Wow, that's fantastic. I'm glad you also did the gluten-free, because I think that's a huge connection there. You know, I get this little brief. I don't know if our caller is familiar with this. There's an autism healing thresholds.com. If you go to autism.healingthresholds.com.

LYNNE GEORGE: I will jot that down.

STUART TOMC: I'm on a list where I get the latest updates. These are integrative approaches to autism, and they talk quite about that gluten-free diet. Again, because what you mentioned with those serotonin cites are primarily in the gut more than the brain; right?

DR. CHRIS: Yea. I mean—well—I mean—what we were—what was interesting to me is that 10% of the neurotransmitters is what we use for cellular communication in the brain. The other 90% were the glial cells which get inflamed due to the adjuvants, and, Stuart, you had some great information about other possible causes here.

STUART TOMC: Yes, there's an emerging theory, which I'm very excited about. You know, we thought for so long that mercury was a problem. We have to make sure to eliminate mercury exposure, and for years, in the fish world, we told pregnant women, "don't eat fish." Right? We're afraid of the prenatal risk of mercury. Then, the NIH recently reversed their position on this, and the preliminary research has been quite exciting. They took a look at a study that was actually conducted in the Sava Islands outside of Madagascar, and they looked at 800 mother-infant pairs from the Sava that ate 12 meals of fish per week. That's a lot of mercury; right, Doc?

DR. CHRIS: Yes, it's about two—two fish meals per day; yea.

STUART TOMC: I mean, this is huge. And, here's a direct quote from *Lancet*[iv], so I don't misquote this, *"[t]hese data do not support the hypothesis that there is any neurodevelopmental risk from prenatal mercury exposure resulting from fish consumption."* So, it then begs the question if the mercury isn't the issue, aren't we sure? May—could it be. I mean, it's the Thiomersal; right? It's the preservative in these vaccines that was directly linked—at least in theory—to skyrocketing autism rates.

DR. CHRIS: Well—

STUART TOMC: Well, two years ago, we removed it, and the rates are still going up!

DR. CHRIS: The rates are still going up, but, Stuart, I beg the question, and this is what I was trying to get through yesterday. When you get to the 50, 60 different adjuvants that make up a vaccine and also the synergy of those adjuvants, couple with the amount of vaccinations that we're doing on children or what the recommended schedule is, which is at least 48 to 54 shots now; okay. And, Brandon, at the time, had seven[v] in one day. So, what is the impact of that synergism that's being created in creating this inflam—inflammatory response here?

STUART TOMC: Well, you make an excellent point. It's those factors rather than the reduction as thinking of it being just the mercury.

DR. CHRIS: I—I

STUART TOMC: —scientists

DR. CHRIS: I think the mercury is a valid point, but I also think in some respects it was also just a rouse to be able to remove the spotlight from these other issues.

STUART TOMC: I—I agree, and I think that that's the risk of that reductionist thinking. It's also brought to light the theory that I shared with you early this morning that PCBs—

DR. CHRIS: Yes.

STUART TOMC: —developed in the 1930s—we heard the word "PCBs." We hear them all them time, but they're actually are? They were coolants. They were oils that were coolants that were used in the nuclear weapons complex, because they were like flame retardants—extremely-high, insulating ability for electric transforms, and they are known endocrine disruptors with tiny amounts in the parts per billion—with a "B"—that negatively affect thyroid function in a developing fetus, with an absolute proven direct link to autism. Overlooked, and I think something we need to focus on a lot more.

DR. CHRIS: I mean, what we're looking at here, Lynne, is giving you ideas and situations of why things may have developed with Brandon and maybe not Anthony here, because they were exposed to the same things; weren't they?

LYNNE GEORGE: They were exposed to the same thing, and Anthony is just total opposite of Brandon. Anthony has scored almost a perfect—he's seven years old, in the second grade. He scored almost a perfect paper on his CRCT test.

DR. CHRIS: Yes.

LYNNE GEORGE: And, he's a straight-A student and everything. He's right on point. But Brandon, he was—he was just delayed, and he even had to go to summer school, because he was so delayed until he even went to extended school this summer.

DR. CHRIS: Yes. So, let's go ahead and take a caller. We have Chrystal from Riverdale with a comment. Good morning, Chrystal. How are you this morning?

RADIO CALLER: [Chrystal] Hi, good morning, Dr. Chris. Thanks for taking my call.

DR. CHRIS: You bet.

RADIO CALLER: [Chrystal] I called you back in the early part of August. My mom was in the ICU unit. She had liver failure. Anyway, we've got her out the hospital thanks to a lot of prayers, and we're going to bringing her in on Friday, but my question today has to do with the whole issue of liver failure, liver disease, and—

DR. CHRIS: Sure.

RADIO CALLER: [Chrystal] What kind of things we can do to, you know, protect the liver and—

DR. CHRIS: Well, I mean, to me, you have to have to stay away from the basic things that we talk about and preach on this show. The refined carbohydrates are just deadly for the liver, and then, of course, the bad fats—the trans fats are just huge, because the liver has to process all of the toxins that your body is exposed to. So, anything that we can do as far as reducing that toxin load is going to be a huge burden that's taken off the liver for the recovery. When I look at the whole picture, I think that there are several things that can be done. Not knowing fully your mother's case, but, I mean, just some of the basic generalities that we look at here. I like to use the protomorphagens, which is the PMG extract that Dr. Lee makes for all the major organs of the body that helps to really facilitate the repair of the particular organ when it has been damaged. I like to do—I would like to make sure that we're consuming large amounts—and I mean, six, seven, eight, nine, ten servings a day of your cruciferous vegetables would not be too much, because those cruciferous vegetables and these sulfur containing compounds are from garlic and onion and eggs have a tremendous affinity for repair of that liver. In fact, they have the substances that help induce and support phase I and phase II liver detoxification. I would also look at some of the herbs that are critical here. Pick rhizome(sp?). You can do the Cynomorium(sp?). And, I mean, there are several things here that I think would be helpful. We also have a Chinese herb that I use, especially for people that have had alcohol drug problems—those type of things where their livers are really damaged. It's called Ecliptek. And that is a complex Chinese herbal formula for the helping to reverse some of the damaging effects of those types of things that are going. Anyone that has liver failure obviously would benefit from that standpoint.

    RADIO CALLER: [Chrystal] Right. I think the root of hers is Hepatitis C.

DR. CHRIS: Okay, Ecliptek falls into that category. Alright. And that is what I would also look at. I would also make sure that her other organs of detoxification, because many times we just focus in—we hear the word "Hepatitis C or B" or whatever it is, and we focus in. Well, we've got to do liver support—liver, liver, liver—but the other thing that we have to keep in mind is what we've learned from other practitioners—Rasovic who is a homeopathic—German homeopathic physician that was brilliant—is that we have to support those other organs of elimination as well. Maybe not do so much liver detoxification, but do more to support kidneys and the bowel and the lungs and the lymphatic and the skin. By doing that, we remove some of the pressure that the liver is going through in being able to the burden of being able to clear some of these toxins out.

    RADIO CALLER: [Chrystal] Right.

DR. CHRIS: In relationship to the hepatitis, I mean, there—you know, that's why I think the protomorphagen is essential. You would want to look at things and other herbs like oregano and olive leaf, you know, in that regard, but also look at the foods that I mention, because that plays a key role in that. As Brenda Watson has said, who has been on this show from her new life. She has Hepatitis C and has had it for a number of years, and she continues to improve, but, I mean, she does a lot of things that, you know, keep her body in check and in shape so that she's able to handle that. Does that help Chrystal?

    RADIO CALLER: [Chrystal] Yes. Definitely.

DR. CHRIS: Anyway. Well, I look forward to seeing you guys on Friday.

RADIO CALLER: [Chrystal] Yes. I'll be looking forward to seeing you as well.

DR. CHRIS: Alright. You take care Chrystal.

RADIO CALLER: [Chrystal] Alright. Thank you so much.

DR. CHRIS: Alright. Bye-bye. Lynne, Stuart—anything you wanted to add in relationship? We understand we have to look at the PCB, which I think is right, but what about as far as Hibba—Hibbawa—is it Hibbawing?

STUART TOMC: Dr. Hiblin.

DR. CHRIS: Hiblin. Man, I'm just like butchering that, Stuart, but that's okay. Hiblan—let's talk about his research in relationship to autism.

STUART TOMC: Well, he's done some, I think, some very, very exciting work, and I had and actual chance to meet him. We've mentioned his name on the show several times, but if you're not familiar with Hiblin's work, it would really behoove anybody interested in the subject of essential fatty acids. This is really the godfather, if you will, of the cutting-edge research. He happens to be the lead clinical investigator for the section of nutritional neurosciences at the Laboratory of Membrane Biophysics and Biochemistry. How is that for a handle, Doc?

DR. CHRIS: Stuart, I'm getting—my eyes are glazing over as you say that. So, explain really in layman's terms what that really means.

STUART TOMC: Well, he's the top researcher. There's a whole department that the National Institutes of Health has that is a special research facility that is dedicated to membrane—cellular member, biophysics and biochemistry.

DR. CHRIS: So, in other words, what effects does the external environment as well as your internal environment have on cell membrane physiology?

STUART TOMC: Which is remarkable that there is an entire department to study that; right?

DR. CHRIS: See, that doesn't even surprise me, because I think that we're just at the beginning of understanding and realizing according to Bruce Lemkin's work that the cell membrane is really truly the brains of the operation of the cell.

STUART TOMC: It is absolutely correct. And, he happens to be a captain in the military and an M.D. with the NIH. So that when this doctors stands up in his captain's uniform, you sort of stand at attention. It's kind of hard to ignore this man; right?

DR. CHRIS: Right. Absolutely.

STUART TOMC: And, he was the one that had published, I think the groundbreaking study that showed the comparison between seafood consumption and homicide rates. He tracked 26 countries around the world and was able to determine that the lower the seafood consumption, thus the lower the omega-3 consumption, the higher** the higher the homicide rate. So, he was really known as quite a maverick in the area of seeing this connection, and he is very concerned about the long-term impact generation-to-generation. This is interesting that we're talking about this young man today. The bioaccumulation of toxicity; right?

DR. CHRIS: Right.

STUART TOMC: And, then the lack of essential fatty acids as we go from generation-to-generation with successive generations of deficiency.

DR. CHRIS: Okay.

STUART TOMC: So, the brain is made up of DHA and oreganonic acids. So, the brain is made up of the essential fatty acids that we don't get unless we get them from our diets.

DR. CHRIS: So, Lynne, that's one of the reasons we put Brandon on cod liver oil is kind of a foundational product there.

STUART TOMC: Which makes absolutely perfect sense, and what Hiblin has recently found out is that the kids who are extremely deficient in omega-3, he said that—this is direct quote, "Frightening data." He has seen the inability of children to make friends, and he also has seen that a lifetime of DHA deficiency can result in a lifetime depression and/or criminal behavior which is even more exacerbated in terms of depression, if you're autistic. He's also finding that children with higher DHA have lower levels of internalizing their problems. So, if you have enough DHA, you're not hanging on to your emotions as much. So, now we're talking EQ—Emotional Intelligence, not just IQ. Higher intelligence at eight. Better math scores and greater non-verbal ability and sentence completion by age 15. So, a lot of incredible research here that Hiblin is doing, and especially when you're looking at the study that Nordic was part of. I don't know if I mentioned this before in the show, Doc, but we were part of the study that was published in the journal of autism and Asperger's digest.

DR. CHRIS: Yes. Let's go ahead and talk about that.

STUART TOMC: Yea. This is a major peer review study that was done that wanted to—to really explore: Could we have a direct influence with autistic children and help them with their language and their learning skills. So, the study was called the benefits of essential fatty acids supplementation. On language and learning skills in children with autism and Asperger's syndrome. Published in *Asperger's and Digest* which is the leading peer review medical journal—conservative medical journal on the subject. This was done at a big pediatric clinic in Tucson, Arizona, and we looked at children with autism or Asperger's syndrome and showed that only two capsules a day, and you probably have them on more than that.

DR. CHRIS: Yea. I think we've been doing the liquid anyway, but go ahead.

STUART TOMC: Two capsules of the 3-6-9 showed—here's the outcome—statistically significant, major improvement in language and learning in both autistic children and children with Asperger's syndrome. So, this is undeniable. When we look at this previously unrecognized interface between innate and adaptive immunity; right? We used to think that this was all a passive process—this resolution of inflammation. Now, we know that it involves active biochemical programs that enable inflamed tissue to return to homeostasis. So, that's why we have influence here, especially in the area of giving the cells back what they need to repair the oxidated damage and to create the neuroprotectants. These are the newly-discovered lipid mediators from Surhan that create like an electric force-field around they synopsis that help protect brain cells from collateral damage from inflammation. If kids are totally deficient in DHA and the immune system is getting tweaked—let's say it's getting tweaked from being over-vaccinated; right? And, then the cells are all wiped out from the immune inflammatory cascade because there isn't enough neuroprotection, that could also be also be a possible link.

DR. CHRIS: Lynne, I mean, to me, you see the influence of the day-to-day things and how all of these things can impact. We've talked about the gluten, we've talked about the lack of these essential fatty acids, which I think, Stuart, it has to be one of the largest deficiencies that we see in the population as a whole right now.

STUART TOMC: I would say that it even out ranks the millions and millions of Americans walking around with unbeknownst sub-clinical scurvy. You know, that's one of our favorite subjects.

DR. CHRIS: Absolutely.

STUART TOMC: And, I saw a recent poll. Ninety-seven percent of Americans are still falling far below 250 or 300 mg of EPA and DHA a day combined.

DR. CHRIS: How many?

STUART TOMC: Ninety-seven percent of Americans—

DR. CHRIS: Ninety-seven percent?

STUART TOMC: —are falling far below—even 250 mg of EPA and DHA a day combined.

DR. CHRIS: Ninety percent of Americans—97% of Americans. Stuart, that means still falling far below 250 or 300 mg of EPA and DHA a day combined.

DR. CHRIS: Stuart, that means you guys have a lot of work to do.

STUART TOMC: We have a lot of work to do, and if I add to that—since we have a little time here—the other captain from the NIH that was there with Dr. Hilbin was looking for a fish oil source for the military. And, he stood there and he says to me, "Sir"—he says to me—"do you know what the EPA/DHA consumption was during the First World War? And I said, look, I'm not a war historian, I don't know. He said, "Well, this is my area of expertise." Hiblin—Dr. Hiblin publishes on the role of essential fatty acids for behavior, and he looks at post-traumatic stress disorder. This is—

DR. CHRIS: Sure.

STUART TOMC: —a fascinating connection here. I did not know this. During the First World War, there were eating sardines and mackerel in cans around the clock, because they could put it in big tubs and seal it, so it wouldn't get poisoned by mustard gas.

DR. CHRIS: Sure. Yea, remember that.

STUART TOMC: So, they were getting 3,000 to 9,000 mg of EPA and DHA a day, combined. He says, "Do you know what the level of post-traumatic stress disorder after post-World War I. He said it was almost non-existent. So, this guy spent his time—this captain, I should call him by his name—this captain doctor—he spent his whole life tracking out over time—looking at all of the different conflicts we've been in and how the level of post traumatic disorder has skyrocketing as the level of essential fatty acid consumption is plummeting.

DR. CHRIS: Wow.

STUART TOMC: Fascinating; isn't it?

DR. CHRIS: It is very fascinating, and this is exactly what we're seeing with our kids today.

STUART TOMC: Exactly.

DR. CHRIS: [INAUDIBLE] They're having problems with anxiety, depression—really looking at self and how they view themselves. A lot of people are having trouble with that.

STUART TOMC: It's true. So, I mean, when you see this connection, when we look at the autoimmune conditions—skyrocketing. When we look at vision degenerating—

DR. CHRIS: Skyrocketing

STUART TOMC: —unresolved resolution of inflammation being connected to all of these things, it's no wonder as our kids are born in more and more toxic soup. I mean, if you look at the work of Doris Rapp,[vi] and if we look at our friend who wrote the "Hundred Year Lie"[vii] and we think of all of these toxic environment. And, I love that statement from the Surgeon General. And I'll say it again—people heard it over and over, but the Surgeon General has now stated that 70% of all death is related to the excess imbalance and deficiency in fat. Now, I'm not saying the only toxic exposure. Seventy percent of it. And, guess what we have total influence over? What we eat. Huge connection here.

DR. CHRIS: Huge connection. Well, Lynne, listen. We have to go to a break. I appreciate you joining us and finishing up this second part of Brandon's odyssey, if you will. And, I think that—what I would hope that we could do is that we again keep following and documenting so we see these little Christmas presents that you're given everyday of Brandon's—what I would call a reawakening.

LYNNE GEORGE: Right. And, I do have one question—

DR. CHRIS: Sure.

LYNNE GEORGE: —for you, Dr. Chris.

DR. CHRIS: Sure go ahead.

LYNNE GEORGE: The pain threshold. That's the part that I'm worried about, but I noticed that it's getting better. Like Brandon—what causes that where Brandon, if he falls, it doesn't bother him?

DR. CHRIS: Well, I think part of that is remember how we were talking about yesterday with the vaccination concept is that it lowers certain levels of it—your body is not responding to inflammation as it is normally would. So, I think that that's part of it. And you have substance "P" level which typically will fluctuate widely. They can either go up or down which control and regulate pain throughout the body.

LYNNE GEORGE: Okay, so it does deal with the inflammation.

DR. CHRIS: Absolutely. So, what we're doing by giving him the nutritional supplements that we're doing, by giving him the infoceuticals, by understanding the probiotics that we're giving him, we're just—we're starting to reestablish that connection. So see, part of the problem, I think, with an autistic child is that there's the cell-to-cell communication is not there.

LYNNE GEORGE: Okay.

DR. CHRIS: You see. And, you do have inflammation, and it may be an overabundance of inflammation that can be creating problems and causing a lack of that cell-to-cell communication, so that when he puts his hand in a fire, he may not feel it initially.

LYNNE GEORGE: Right, it's like a delayed reaction.

DR. CHRIS: Delayed reaction, but that's because of the lack of the cell-to-cell communication. And now what you're seeing probably is that his pain threshold is starting to normalize.

LYNNE GEORGE: Right. Because he'll knock himself or fall down, and then it's like he'll think for a second—a few seconds—and all of a sudden, he'll come to me like, and you know, hold like whatever it is, and, you know—

DR. CHRIS: Be in pain.

LYNNE GEORGE: Exactly.

DR. CHRIS: And, that's a good sign. That's a real good sign. Lynne, wonderful. I know that you're going to be writing a book. We're going to be having you back on—just giving us updates on this. I appreciate you being with us.

LYNNE GEORGE: And, thank you, Dr. Chris, and thank you, Stuart.

STUART TOMC: Oh, my pleasure. And, I hope you wrote down the website there about the autism briefs.

LYNNE GEORGE: I sure did.

DR. CHRIS: Okay.

STUART TOMC: Because, you can contact them and share your story—

DR. CHRIS: That's going to be huge. We've got to get this word out; okay.

STUART TOMC: Because this goes out to all of the integrated physicians and all the practitioners that can make a difference.

LYNNE GEORGE: Oh, that's great.

STUART TOMC: And you keep detailed notes of what Dr. Chris is putting him on, and we can track this and help other people break this terrible cycle.

DR. CHRIS: That's what we want. Lynne, as always, thank you very much.

LYNNE GEORGE: Thank you, Dr. Chris.

DR. CHRIS: Alright. You take care.

LYNNE GEORGE: Alright.

DR. CHRIS: Stuart, we're going to take a quick break. Tony, we're going to cue it up here. We're going to be back. We've got some major news to cover about fish oil against heart failure. 678—excuse me, 770-491-7748. You're listening to "To Your Health with Dr. Chris." We'll be back right after this.

[Music interlude]

[THE END]

---

[i] Stuart Tomc is an authority on evidence-based dietary supplements with over twenty years experience in the field of Nutritional Medicine. He is a respected consultant to the World Health Organization and integrative physicians worldwide having traveled the world as an educator and trainer for over 10 years. Stuart is adept at educating and delivering a powerful message on important health issues and currently serves as National Educator and Spokesperson for Nordic Naturals. (*See* www.nordicnaturals.com.)

[ii] Dr. Daniel Falor earned his BA degree at the University of New York, and then went on to earn his Doctorate of Chiropractic degree from Life Chiropractic College in Marietta, Georgia. After graduating, Dr. Falor was Clinic Director of a successful practice in Loganville, Georgia. In addition to his Chiropractic degree, Dr. Falor has advanced certifications in

Nambudripad's Allergy Elimination Technique (NAET), Body Restoration Technique (BRT) and Contact Reflex Analysis (CRA). He has also studied extensively in the field of nutrition and uses many Homeopathic remedies in his quest to provide the best in all-natural health care to his patients. Dr. Falor is pleased to have joined with Dr. Chris Greene at Dr. Chris' Natural Pharmacy, their combined extensive knowledge of nutrition and homeopathy will bring unmatched natural health and wellness care to everyone in the greater Atlanta area. Holistic Health Restoration, 11100 Donnington Drive, Duluth, GA 30097, Tel: (770) 401-6065, Email: drfalor@msn.com.

[iii] Laurie Ledbetter is the US distributor for Dr. Natasha Campbell-McBride's book, "Gut and Psychology Syndrome" and her Biokult. (*See* website: http://www.guthealth.info.)

[iv] *Lancet* is a UK medical journal.

[v] *See* Brandon's Certificate of Immunizations (clarification of the number of shots administered to Brandon).

[vi] Doris J. Rapp, M.D., F.A.A.A., F.A.A.P., is a board-certified environmental medical specialist and pediatric allergist, and a New York Times bestselling author who has appeared on Oprah and many other nationally televised talk shows. She is clinical assistant professor of pediatrics at the State University of New York at Buffalo. She is the founder of the Practical Allergy Foundation in Buffalo and is a past president of the American Academy of Environmental Medicine. (Source: Random House, Inc.)

[vii] Samuel S. Epstein, M.D. (Professor emeritus Environmental & Occupational Medicine, University of Illinois at Chicago, School of Public Health, and Chairman, Cancer Prevention Coalition) wrote: "Randall Fitzgerald's book is a classic. Rather than 'better living through chemistry,' the book reveals how the totality of our environment, including water, processed food, and pharmaceuticals have become permeated with innumerable toxic synthetic chemicals. The scientific basis for these conclusions is well documented and impeccable. This information is presented in a highly readable and gripping style. The book should be on every concerned citizens' shelf." (*See* www.hundredyearlie.com)

CPSIA information can be obtained at www.ICGtesting.com
Printed in the USA
241177LV00002B/127/P